GW00370427

R I G H T
RICHES
for You

Evan

I gift you this
book, It contains
a lot of wisdom
you can
choose
to use
mum
xxxxx

6/2013

RIGHT
RICHES
for You

Gary M. Douglas & Dr. Dain Heer

Big Country Publishing, LLC

Right Riches For You
Copyright© 2010, 2012 by Gary M. Douglas & Dr. Dain C. Heer
Library of Congress Control Number: 2012933920
ISBN: 978-0-9847831-6-8
eBook ISBN: 978-0-9847831-8-2

Cover design by Kyle Petrove
Cover image ©dreamstime.com 4427306
First Printing 2010

All rights reserved. No part of this publication may be reproduced, stored in a retrieval system, or transmitted, in any form or by any means electronic, mechanical, photocopying, recording, or otherwise without prior written permission from the publisher. The author and publisher of the book do not make any claim or guarantee for any physical, mental, emotional, spiritual, or financial result. All products, services and information provided by the author are for general education and entertainment purposes only. The information provided herein is in no way a substitute for medical or other professional advice. In the event you use any of the information contained in this book for yourself, the author and publisher assume no responsibility for your actions. Big Country Publishing, LLC accepts no responsibility or liability for any content, bibliographic references, artwork, or works cited contained in this book.

Published by
Big Country Publishing, LLC
7691 Shaffer Parkway, Suite C
Littleton, CO 80127
USA
www.bigcountrypublishing.com

Printed in the United States of America
International printing in the U.K. and Australia

Table of Contents

Changing the Way You View Things

What Does Money Mean to You?

The Four Elements of Generating Wealth

Be Willing to Have Money

Generate Money

Changing the Way
You View Things

Changing the Way You View Things

If you're like most people, you have many points of view about money that you're not even aware you have. These points of view are the cause of many of your so-called money problems. In this book, Dain and I would like to present some ways of thinking about money that will encourage you to see your financial world in a different way. We'd like to help you change the points of view that keep you from having money with ease and comfort.

This book is about generating a financial reality that is far greater than the one you already have. We'll talk about what it takes to actually have money as opposed to getting money. We'll also discuss how to generate money in your life, and we'll provide you with tools you can use to make the current economic meltdown into a success. We'll suggest ways of making money out of these conditions instead of having your money made off with. It's all about looking at things from a slightly different point of view.

We want to give you the opportunity to recognize that there may be a different way of looking at the world. And there may be a way to generate something totally different in your life if you change the way you view things.

What Does Money Mean To You?

T o begin, here are two short exercises that will help you discover what money means to you.

What Does Money Mean to You?

Write down your answers to the question, "What does money mean to you?"

_____

_____

_____

_____

_____

Consider Your Answers

Look at each of the answers you wrote in response to the question. Does it make you feel lighter to think that this is what money is? Or does it make you feel heavier? If something makes you feel lighter, it is true for you. If it makes you feel heavier, it's a lie.

To give you an idea of how this exercise might go, here are some answers people gave in a recent money class:

Gary: Okay, the first answer is sex. So, is money sex? Does that make you feel lighter or heavier?

Participant: Heavier.

Gary: Heavier. Okay, good. The next answer is opportunity. Is money opportunity? Does that make you feel lighter or heavier?

Participant: Lighter.

Gary: Okay, lighter. Opportunity is one of the elements of the energy of money.

The next one is security. Does that make you feel lighter or heavier? Heavier, because security is not something that you can have at all. Ask anyone who lives in San Francisco how secure he or she feels. At any moment, the ground under his or her feet is likely to open up and swallow them. And you think you have security? Get over yourself. You're crazy!

The next answer is freedom. Money is freedom. Does it make you feel lighter or heavier?

Participant: Heavier.

Gary: Yes, heavier. Freedom does not come from money. Money comes with freedom. What if your life was not about what you thought you were going to get with money? What if it was about the awareness that money comes to you as a result of choosing that which is freeing to you?

There are a lot of people who say, "You have to follow your passion." If you look up the word passion in an old dictionary, you will see that it means to be tacked to the cross as Christ was. Following your passion doesn't get you where you want to go. But if you do what you love, money comes along for the ride. You have to be willing to do what you love.

Dain: When you're willing to have freedom of choice, you generate or create the money. People think money is going to give them freedom, but it's actually the other way around. The willingness to have freedom allows the money to show up.

Gary: When you are willing to choose, then money will come. The next answer is relaxation. Money is relaxation. Does that make you feel lighter or heavier? Heavier. Money is not relaxation. You might feel more relaxed when you have more money in your bank account, but that's not what money is. The next one is choice. Is money choice? Does that make you feel light or heavy?

Participant: Heavy.

Gary: Yes, because money isn't choice, but choice generates money. What you choose generates money, but money doesn't give you choice.

Dain: Choice is similar to the concept of freedom. If you're willing to have freedom as part of your life, you'll generate freedom no matter what it looks like. If it takes money for me to have freedom, cool, I'll have money. If it takes lots of roses around me, I'll have roses. You know what generates freedom for you. It's the same with money. If you're willing to have the things that generate money, then you'll have money. Many people think of money as the source of things instead of recognizing it's the other way around. Choice isn't money. Choice is the source of money. Choice creates awareness. Awareness does not create choice.

Gary: Choice is the source for everything in your life. Choice generates all opportunities and all possibilities. Choice generates everything that is possible in your life. Choice is the source. The things you choose are the source for what occurs in your life.

Now look at each of the answers you wrote in response to the question, "What does money mean to you?" Does your answer make you feel lighter? Does it correctly define money for you? Or does it make you feel heavier? If your answer is true for you, you'll feel lighter. If it's not true for you, you'll feel heavier. Much of what you have bought from others about money is what makes you feel heavy.

In our view, money is a vehicle. That's what it really is. All the other things on the list like security, relaxation, freedom, and so on are what people thought money was. Do you see that if you look at money from a point of view that isn't truly yours, it might seem different from what it actually is?

For example, look at a wall in the room where you're sitting. That's a wall. Is it a pretty wall, an ugly wall, a perfect wall, a right wall, a good wall, or is it just a wall? It's just a wall. Can you get over the idea that the wall is pretty or ugly? It's the same with money. We say, "Good money. Bad money. Right money. Wrong money. Right way to get money. Wrong way to get money." Those are all judgments. They don't have anything to do with what money is; they are simply things you've decided based on your good or bad experiences and what you've been taught or what you've bought from others.

Throughout the book, we offer questions, processes, and other tools you can use to become aware of the points of view you have about money and clear them out of your space. We hope you will use them to create a different financial reality for yourself.

You, The Infinite Being

Some people have been told or taught that they need to get a concept of what they desire so they can have the things they would like to have. What's a concept? It's a map, a picture, a how-to, or a definition. It is something the mind creates. The idea of getting a concept of what you desire may have some limited workability, but the universe is amazingly more vast and unlimited than anything your mind can comprehend or create—and its possibilities are boundless. Why would you want to use your mind to create your life in the same limited way you have been? Why would you want to map out tomorrow the day before you get there so you know what you are going to do? Why would you want to operate in a way that automatically limits what is available to you?

There is a completely different way of viewing things—and a completely different way of operating in the universe. It starts with recognizing who we are. We are infinite beings. Did you realize that? As infinite beings, we have the infinite ability to perceive, know, be, and receive, but rather than recognizing that we are infinite and functioning as the infinite beings we truly are, we've done a lot over the last 4 trillion years to make ourselves terribly finite. Lifetime after lifetime we come back, and each time we return, we become more and more finite in our points of view until infinite isn't even a concept we can grasp. We actually deny our infinite nature. Often we do this so we can be in agreement with everyone else in our world. We say, "This is the way my mom does it, so this is the way I'll do it" or "This is not something my friends would understand or agree with, so I'm not going to have that any more." When we do things like that, we cut ourselves off from our own infinite nature, and from the infinite possibilities that are available to us.

We function with far less power, ability, joy, fun, money—you name it—than we could have. Dain told me, "Before I got into Access, I used to hear people say that we are infinite beings, and I'd think, 'I'm an infinite being? If that's true, then why does my life look the way it does? Shouldn't an infinite being at least be able to pay the rent? Shouldn't an infinite being wake up happy every now and again? Shouldn't an infinite being actually like his life? If I'm so infinite, why the hell does my life look the way it does?' "

It's because instead of choosing to perceive everything, know everything, and be everything—which allows us to receive everything, including all the money we could ever ask for—we choose to operate within the limitations of this reality. We choose to be in agreement with everyone else about what is. We reject what we could have. We refuse to receive it. We believe we have to part and parcel ourselves like everybody else does. We reduce ourselves down; we limit ourselves. We define ourselves in terms of our body, our bank account, or the house we live in. We try to make ourselves like everybody else so we fit in.

The reality is we are everything, but we say, "Oh no, I'm a finite being. I am limited by the size of my body or the pond that I live in." We get stuck in the lie, "I am a very limited being. I'm finite in my capacity." It's not true. We are not limited and finite!

You, as a being, are nothing but a cool, spring breeze. You are just space. You are not your body. These bodies are limited, but you, on the other hand, are everything. How can you put you, who are infinite, into a body? You can't. Actually, your body is inside you. Your body functions inside of you, not you inside your body. Even if you made your body weigh 1,000 pounds, it still wouldn't be big enough to contain you.

Close your eyes and find the outside edges of you.

You, the being.

Can you find the outside edges of you?

Or is everywhere you look, where you are?

That's an infinite being.

Could a being that big fit inside a body this small?

Isn't your body actually inside of you?

When a situation shows up in your life that isn't working for you, try asking, "Would an infinite being choose this? No? Then why am I?" If an infinite being wouldn't choose it, why would you? We invite you to look at those places where you decided a limitation was a good thing and unlock them, so you don't have to maintain that point of view any more. You don't have to take on the limited points of view that other people buy into. You can choose differently.

Do you have any idea of what it would be like to live your life moment-by-moment as the infinite being you truly are? Well, for one thing, you would claim and own that you are an infinite being with infinite powers. You wouldn't buy into the agreements of this reality. You'd have too much to do! You'd be having too much fun. And you'd probably have too much money!

Chapter 2

Receiving

Abundance is not about the amount of money you have in your bank account. It's about having more of everything in your life. It's about having joy in your life. Abundance is about everything that you are willing to receive.

Dain and I have worked with all kinds of people about their so-called money issues. It doesn't matter whether they had $10—or $10 million; they have all had the same money issue. How can this be? It's because money isn't the problem; the problem is their unwillingness to receive. They are unable to receive, there are things they don't want to receive, or they don't believe it is good to receive. It is what you are unwilling to receive in life that keeps you from having the money you would like to have.

Most people are more comfortable with not having money than they are with having money. They seem to have the point of view that if you have a lot of money, it means you have stolen from somebody else, you've used others badly, or you are totally depraved. So they will deprive themselves in order not to be depraved. They choose deprivation rather than depravity.

I am willing to generate a lot of money. Some people might think I don't deserve it, and they may be right—but even so, I am willing to receive it. Most people can only have what they think they deserve. But do you deserve to feel the cool wind on a hot day—or do you just feel it? Do you deserve to have the sun on your face—or do you just go outdoors and there it is? What if money was like the sun? What if it were something that shines down on you? What if it came to you as easily as the flow of your breath? This is the way it is supposed to be! Receiving is supposed to be like receiving the air you breathe, the warmth of the sun, and the caress of the wind.

Addiction to Poverty

Many of the people we work with suffer from an addiction to poverty, which is the unwillingness to let everything in the universe gift to them. If you wish to have money, you must be willing to receive. You must be willing to allow everything in the world to gift to you. The limits of your reality are based on the amount of money you are willing to allow yourself to have. In other words, if you are willing to have just enough money, you will always be just a paycheck away from poverty; you will continually create that financial reality. If you are only willing to have slightly more than you actually need, then you will continually create that. That becomes the limitation of your reality. If you think that you have to work hard in order to have money and you don't have a sense of ease with it, then you will constantly create that as your reality.

Many years ago when I had no money, I would go around to garage sales to buy things I could sell to earn extra money. One day when I was out, I saw a 14-carat gold doorknob priced at $4. At that time, it would have been worth about $1,000. On that particular day, I didn't have any cash. I had my checkbook, but my wife at the time had written checks we didn't have the money to cover, and I had committed myself to never writing a check that was bad. I was so committed to not writing bad checks that I couldn't even see the opportunity in front of me. That is a sad thing—and I am a smart guy. I should have known better. If that happened today, I wouldn't say, "Oh no, I can't do this!" I would look at the opportunity and ask, "Okay, how can I get the money?"

This is something we all do in our lives. We say, "I can't do that." Instead, ask, "What will it take to make this work?" It is a different point of view that you've got to begin to function from if you truly wish to generate and create wealth. Don't refuse money and the things you would like to have in your life because of your addiction to poverty.

Be Willing to Receive Everything

If you really wish to have money, you have to be willing to receive everything. We mean everything, the good and the bad, the beautiful and the ugly. It doesn't mean you have to choose to have that thing in your life—but you have to be willing to receive it. You have to be willing to receive any energy, whatever the energy is. The willingness to receive means you recognize that all things can come to you, and they don't stick with you. They keep on going. Does energy ever stop? No.

When you don't like something or you think it's wrong, you cut off the energy of that thing—and energy is the source of everything in our lives. It's what creates every possibility. When we're not willing to receive something, we stop energy from coming to us, and we cut ourselves off from the energy of the universe. Everything we've decided we can't receive equals the inability to receive money. If you decide, "I don't like blondes," then you won't be able to receive money from anyone who has blond hair. If you're a moralist, you won't be willing to receive from people who are not moral.

Once you realize that everything is part of your universe, you get to choose what you would like to have. That's different from rejecting things that you judge as bad or undesirable. When you try to reject things from your universe, you are unable to receive anything, including money. Get the energy of judging someone else— or judging yourself. What does that feel like? Does your life expand or contract when you're in the throes of that judgment? It contracts. Your life swallows itself up when you judge. You go into your own personal black hole. When you're in that state, what are you willing to receive from others? Nothing. You deny the possibility of anyone or anything contributing money to you.

You have to be able to receive everything, even others' judgments of you. Judgment is something that many people don't want to receive; they don't want people to judge them. They refuse to receive judgment. But a judgment is not a truth. Does someone think you're ugly or beautiful, fat or thin, lazy or a workaholic? So what? It's just their judgment. Every time you're willing to receive somebody's judgment—not make it real, but receive it—you'll receive another $5,000 that year. You've got to be willing to receive judgment, as well as everything else, if you're going to have money.

The British entrepreneur, Richard Branson, who is one of the richest people in the world, is willing to receive all kinds of judgment. The reality is if you're going to have lots of money, you are going to receive lots of judgment. People judge you for having money, because, as they say in Australia, "You cut down the tall poppies." This means you don't want to stand out from the crowd because people will cut you down. People with huge amounts of money get all kinds of judgment, but if they're like Richard Branson and they don't have a judgment about others' judgments being real, they don't cut themselves off from having money. Allow yourself to receive others' judgments. Their point of view about you is nothing but their point of view. Don't resist it or react to it, don't accept it or reject it. Just say, "Hm. That's an interesting point of view."

A lady told me that she was walking down Market Street in San Francisco, and she saw a homeless man sitting in the street. Her usual reaction would have been to resist him, as well as her own fear that she might become homeless someday. But instead of doing that, she said to herself, "I'm going to totally receive him and the fact that I could be sitting there with him." When she did this, her fear of being homeless went "poof." She said, "I realized being homeless was part of my universe, like everything else, but I knew I didn't have to choose to be homeless."

One of my favorite examples about the importance of being able to receive everything happened when I was working with a man who had a clothing store in a gay section of Houston. His business wasn't making money, and he said to me, "I need some help. I don't know what's going on, but my business is failing." I went to the store and I looked at his merchandise. Everything looked good. I looked at his books, and there wasn't anything wrong. He didn't have everything upside down. I said, "Tell me about your customers." He said, "Well most of them are pretty good, but there are those people I don't like."

I asked, "What do you mean, those people?"

He said, "You know, those swishy guys."

I said, "Oh, you have a clothing store in a gay section of town, and you don't like swishy guys? Who shops in the gay section of town? Do straight men shop in the gay section of town? No. Do the wives of straight guys go to a store in a gay section of town? No. You'd better decide you like those people. They're your customers."

He said, "Yeah, but I hate it when they hit on me."

I asked, "Do you ever hit on women?"

He said, "Well, not when my wife's around."

Then I asked, "Do you expect to get laid when you hit on them?"

He said, "No, I just like to flirt."

I asked, "Well, what if those guys just like to flirt with you?"

He said, "Oh, I could never have that."

I replied, "Well, you're going to have to learn to have that if you want your business to succeed. I'm going to be the swishy man who's hitting on you, and you're going to learn to talk to me."

So I started out with, "Oh sweetie, these are such beautiful clothes," and he just about came unglued.

I continued, "You know, I'd just love to have sex with you."

And he said, "Oh my God!"

After about forty-five minutes of working with him, he got to the point where he could start to flirt back. He started to enjoy playing with the energy, and within two months his business became totally successful. Just because someone flirts with you and you flirt with them doesn't mean you have to copulate. It doesn't mean you have to carry through. It doesn't mean anything except that you're willing to receive the energy.

Someone asked me, "If you're around dangerous people or crazy people, how can you receive them?"

I said, "That's easy. Know they're crazy. Know they're dangerous. You wouldn't pick them up in your car and you wouldn't take them home. Just be totally aware and have no judgment of them." I don't have judgments about people, and because of that, I can receive money from anyone. This doesn't mean I have to deal with all of those people. It simply means I am willing to receive their energy.

A woman who heard the story about the man with the clothing store asked me, "What do you do when you're receiving a man's energy of lust and then he starts to follow it up with a touch?"

I advised her to say, "Sweetheart, if you do that again, I'm going to cut your dick off."

She said, "Yes, but ten seconds ago you were talking about receiving and telling us to flirt!"

I answered, "You are receiving. You've just received the information that he's an asshole. Just because you flirted or went out to dinner with somebody doesn't mean you have to go to bed with them."

Women always have control. They get to say, "Come here. No. Come here. No." When a man touches, he's gone too far. It's amazing how many guys are used to getting away with that kind of behavior.

When this happens, take control. You say, "If you do that again I'll cut off your testicles." When you say something like this to them, all of a sudden, they really like you. They respect you. They've wanted somebody to put them in their place for an awfully long time, and you had the potency to do it. You have to be willing to receive whatever energy there is, but that doesn't mean you have to do anything in exchange for it. It doesn't mean you have to take it in the shorts. Receiving everything doesn't mean you become a doormat.

If you wish to be truly abundant and to have everything—including outrageous amounts of money—you have to be willing to receive everything. You also have to be willing to be, do, have, create, and generate everything in life. Anything else is functioning from judgment, which cuts off your ability to be and receive everything.

Chapter 3

Living in the Question

Contextual Reality vs. Non-Contextual Reality

What Dain and I call contextual reality is a limited point of view of the universe. It's about how you win, how you lose… Contextual reality is actually just 10 percent of the universe—but it's the universe most people live in and operate from. When you say, "I can't do this" or "This isn't working," you are functioning in contextual reality. The only time you get upset, the only time you worry, is when you're in contextual reality.

Contextual reality defines limitations in life. It's the judgment system of this reality—because it requires judgment to determine whether you are winning or losing and whether you are fitting or benefiting. Huge amounts of people are doing contextual reality, so you can't get rid of it. You can't destroy it, and you can't live outside of it. You have to be able to live with it. But you don't have to live in it! You can live in the non-contextual universe or non-contextual reality. Non-contextual reality is about awareness, possibilities, and choices. It's about questions: "Okay, what are the possibilities here? What questions can I ask? What choices do I have? What contribution can I be?" When you ask, "How could this show up

29

as something even greater than I can imagine?" you're functioning in non-contextual reality. If contextual reality is 10 percent of the universe, non-contextual reality makes up the other 990 percent.

The 1996 movie Phenomenon is a great example of non-contextual reality. The main character, played by John Travolta, functions from the non-contextual universe. Everything is available to him. A lot of people find him weird because of his abilities—and when you start to function from your abilities, people may find you weird as well. You have to be willing to be considered the weird one, or you can't function in the full 1000 percent of the universe. The universe is providing you with incredible opportunities. When you open yourself to non-contextual reality, you bring these possibilities into your life. How do you do this? One of the most important things you can do to begin living in non-contextual reality and to change your financial world—and all of your life—is to live in the question.

Living in the question means inviting the universe to support you by asking unlimited questions. Everything in the universe is conscious, and every molecule that exists will help support you. Science tells us that when we look at a molecule, we change its structure—just by the act of looking at it. The consciousness of molecules contributes to us; contribution is part of their nature. If we don't understand that we have an impact on every molecule we come into contact with, we will not allow molecules to contribute to us—and we will not receive what molecules are trying to give us.

Living in the question is the opposite of trying to figure things out. When you try to work out the way you are going to make something happen, you go into figuring out the answer rather than inviting the universe to provide infinite possibilities. Don't try to figure things out. Your mind is a dangerous thing. It can only define what you already know. It cannot be infinite and unlimited. Whenever you have an answer, that's the sum total of what can show up for you. But when you ask an unlimited question like, "What would it take for ____ to show up?" you invite the universe to support you in ways you haven't even imagined.

Throughout this book, we offer many different questions and processes you can use to change the way you view the world, thereby freeing up your ability to generate unlimited amounts of money. To start, we'll talk about the specific ways in which you develop points of view that limit the amount of money you have in your life, and how you can use questions to clear them out of your space.

Evidentiary Contrivances

It's not what is in the world that determines what your life is like, because the world doesn't have a point of view. It is the other way around. The world supports your point of view of it. Another way of saying this is that your point of view creates your reality. Your reality doesn't create your point of view. Are you aware of that? For example, if you have the point of view that it's a struggle to get money, you will always have a struggle in your universe regarding money. People who buy this viewpoint from their parents continue to have money struggles unless they undo their stuck viewpoints about money. The expression "shirt sleeves to shirt sleeves in three generations" expresses the idea that you can't be greater than what you were raised to be.

We met a man in Tennessee who expressed this idea in another way. In a strong Southern accent, he said, "You can't go above your raisin'." I thought, "Hm. What does that mean?" I imagined a muffin with a raisin on top. Then I realized he was saying, "You can't go above the way you were raised." If you are raised in poverty, you assume that poverty is normal and correct. If you were raised in the middle class, you assume that being middle class is normal and correct. You adopt the points of view of the people around you—and then you create your reality based on your point of view.

Most people set up their lives based on the evidentiary contrivances they've had from the time that they were little. An evidentiary contrivance is a contrived point of view. It's a viewpoint you have developed.

31

It is when you say, "This is the way money ought to be," or "This is the way things work with money." You consider that something is a certain way and then you gather evidence to try and make it right. You are not looking at what is. You are looking at the way you would like something to be or the way you decided things are.

For example, have you ever been in a relationship with somebody and become so focused on how you wanted that person to be that you couldn't see how he or she really was? "Oh, I love them! They're so wonderful." Yeah, they're wonderful—except when they're mean, nasty, and awful to you. If you are focused on what you want them to be and on how you want the relationship to work out instead of seeing how they really are and what the relationship actually is, you'll go around saying things like, "Well, it's going to work out eventually." The evidence doesn't support the picture you have contrived. That's an evidentiary contrivance.

Let's say you have the point of view, "The only way I can get money is by working a nine-to-five job." You pull this point of view out of the air—or you pull it out of your parents' heads—and you decide, "This is the way it is." Then you start looking for evidence that proves the point of view you contrived is actually true. You begin to create your life to prove the rightness of that viewpoint. Do you look beyond the narrow evidence that seems to confirm your point of view? No. You are not functioning from awareness. You are functioning from an evidentiary contrivance.

A friend of ours told us that her father turned down the vice presidency of an oil company to become a professor. The evidentiary contrivance in her family was that education was everything and that only "crude" people had money. They were out to prove the superiority of having no money.

Dain had a version of this in his family. He says that in his family, the evidentiary contrivance was, "We may not have money, but unlike those rich people, we're happy." He didn't buy into this one.

His reaction was, "Excuse me, but have you looked at yourself lately? Is this what you call happy? I'd rather have some money and try out the other side. It can't be any less happy than you guys are."

A man we know told us he had been "occasionally happy" during his forty-two years of marriage. He said his parents were married for sixty-eight years, and he had decided he should be able to do that as well. He created the same kind of marriage situation his parents had—long lasting, but not very happy. He decided a long-lasting marriage was a good thing, and then he tried to create that reality—no matter what.

In order to make something right that isn't, we back it up with the evidence we gather to prove the rightness of our point of view. Evidentiary contrivances are interesting points of view that demonstrate the rightness of all the limitations in your life. Every limitation in your life is based on evidentiary contrivance. Everyone.

One of the things we want more than anything else is to hold on to the rightness of our point of view, even if it isn't working for us. Evidentiary contrivances are more dynamic, more contractive, more intense, and more limiting than anything else in our existence. If there is any place where your life is not changing the way you would like it to, you have an evidentiary contrivance—or a few million of them—holding it in place.

If there is some area of your life you can't seem to change, ask, "How many evidentiary contrivances do I have holding this in place?" Then use a clearing statement: "Right and Wrong, Good and Bad, POD, and POC, All Nine, Shorts, Boys and Beyonds.™" It's not necessary to look for an answer. The question brings up the energy, and then the clearing statement goes to the point of creation where you made the evidentiary contrivance, or to the point of destruction, where you destroyed some part of your awareness or your consciousness in order to hold a limited point of view in place, and it erases them so you can have a different possibility. It doesn't matter whether the point of creation or destruction was last week or a hundred million years ago. The clearing statement takes you to the first place it happened and clears the decisions you made. It happens energetically when you use the question and the clearing statement.

There is more information at the back of this book about the clearing statement, but it's not necessary to understand it for it to work. When you get to the point where you actually care about knowing what it is, you can look it up or go to an Access class and ask someone to explain it to you.

Conflictual Universes

Many people hate money—and you might be one of them. If you don't have very much money in your life, it's likely that you hate money. If you were willing to love money, you'd probably have a lot more of it, and you'd have an easier time in life. Were you told as a child that the love of money is the root of evil? And are you refusing to be evil? But would you also love to have more money? This creates a conundrum, doesn't it? It's what we call a conflictual universe, a conflictual reality, or a conflictual paradigm.

> Everything you've done to equate money with evil, and evil with money, and all the ways you've tried to not be evil as a way of making sure that you're not going to have money, will you destroy and uncreate all of that? Right and Wrong, Good and Bad, POD, POC, All Nine, Shorts, Boys and Beyonds.

All you have to do with the question, "Will you destroy and uncreate all of that?" is say yes—but make sure you really mean yes. A lot of people say yes when they really mean no. Your willingness to change it begins the process of change. Then say the clearing statement, which energetically clears your limitations.

Decisions, Judgments, Computations or Conclusions (DJCCs)

Have you decided what will—and what will not—make you money? Have you decided what's good—and what's not? There is a big problem connected with making decisions, judgments, computations, and conclusions (DJCCs). Any decision, judgment, computation, or conclusion will limit what you can have.

Anytime you make a decision, judgment, computation, or conclusion, you have to "prove" the rightness of it. Let's say you're working hard to achieve something; or example, a new business. You reach a place where you think everything is going to work out the way you envisioned—but then it doesn't. You come to a conclusion, "This didn't work."

When you conclude, "This didn't work," you stop the energy you've been using to generate whatever you wished to have, and you have to start over again to build something else. And then when that doesn't come to fruition, once again you decide, "That didn't work," and the whole cycle begins once more. "That didn't work" is a DJCC. It stops the energy. You reach a conclusion, and that's all that can show up. Everything you were generating falls apart. It puts you into a continuous create-and-destroy cycle.

Instead of doing a DJCC like "that didn't work," you need to ask a question. You say, "Hm. That didn't turn out the way I wanted. What else is possible?" Instead of making DJCCs like "I've got that handled" or "This is the right choice" or "This is the way things are," you need to live in the question.

Many of us choose what feels familiar or comfortable. But if you're choosing only what feels familiar and comfortable, you're going to get the same result ten years from now that you've always gotten. You'll continue to choose the same things you have always chosen, and you will continue to get the same result you have always gotten. What if you were willing to step out of your comfort zone? DJCCs contribute to creating the comfort zone you function from. Unfortunately, these DJCCs also create a huge limitation in your life regarding money.

An interesting thing about Richard Branson is that he never comes to a conclusion. When something doesn't work out the way he wishes, he asks, "What can I do different that will create a different result?" The willingness to look at what else you can create and what you can do that will create a different result will keep you in the forward motion of creating money and having money.

How many decisions, judgments, computations, and conclusions (DJCCs) do you have that limit the amount of money you can have in your life? Will you destroy and uncreate all of that? Right and Wrong, Good and Bad, POD, POC, All Nine, Shorts, Boys and Beyonds.

Trying to Turn a Decision Into a Truth. In one of our classes, we worked with a woman who kept saying, "I'm frigging poor."

I asked her, "What question is that?"

As we talked, it became clear to her that she was living her life from a decision that she was trying to turn into a truth. "I'm frigging poor" is not a truth! It's a bad decision. She was trying to make her bad decisions into a truth.

Have you made your decision about your financial situation a truth? Everything that is, will you destroy and uncreate it all? Right and Wrong, Good and Bad, POD, POC, All Nine, Shorts, Boys and Beyonds.

Another lady in one of our classes asked me, "Could you help me with something I don't understand? After I started doing Access last year, I made more money, more easily than I ever have in my life. I threw some limitations out the window and after that, I started generating a lot of money. Then all of a sudden, everything came to a screeching halt. It was boom! No more money. I don't understand what happened."

After we talked for a while, she realized that she had decided, "Okay! I've finally got it. I know how to do this now."

As soon as you think, "I've got it," you stop the energy flows and you stop the income. Why is that? Because you've stopped the energy that was generating what was possible. Initially she was committed to generating the energy of money and she was asking questions, but then she moved over to "I've got it." Is there a question in "I've got it"? No. Is "I've got it" inviting the energy of the universe to help you? No. It's a decision. It's telling the universe you don't require its contribution any longer. If you aren't willing to ask questions, the universe cannot contribute to you. But when you live in the question, the universe will take care of you.

Another variety of DJCCs are statements with a question mark attached. They're not really questions. Sometimes people draw a conclusion and then phrase their conclusion as if it were a question. But even if you put a question mark at the end of a statement, it's still a statement.

After one of our classes, a woman had a headache and concluded that the headache resulted from the class. She asked, "What's wrong that I have a headache?" Is this a question? No. It's a statement with a question mark attached. Once we delved into what was going on, she realized she just needed to relax and move her body. She saw that her body needed to lighten up and go swimming, but she didn't even think of doing this because she had decided something was wrong. She jumped to a conclusion. She didn't ask a question. She didn't inquire, "Body, what do you need?" Your body is a sensing organism. Its job is to give you information. When you draw conclusions about your body without asking it what it needs, the headache or whatever information you are receiving from it in the form of sensations, will intensify. The sensations continue to worsen as your body tries to give you information about what it requires. If something is getting continuously worse, it means you've made a DJCC or an evidentiary contrivance. Go back and undo that by using the clearing statement, and then start asking questions. When I have a problem with my body, I ask it, "Body, what do you need?" I start with water, salt, and sugar. If it says, "Water," I ask, "Drink it? Swim in it? Submerge myself in it? Shower?" My body always lets me know what it needs—if I ask it a question.

Issues That Don't Belong to You

Sometimes we take on issues that aren't even ours, and we try as hard as we can to handle them. Does this work? Can we handle them? No! The issue doesn't belong to us. When Dain was about thirteen, he started trying to handle "his" money issue. Years later, after he began doing Access, he discovered that what he thought was his money issue wasn't even his. It didn't belong to him. It was his father's. His dad had a business that was failing, so his father's money issue became the family's money issue, and Dain kept trying to handle it as though it was his issue. Dain thought he was a failure with money. In other words, he adopted his dad's point of view about money, which was that life was about the money you didn't make and the money you didn't have.

Dain bought the "failure with money" point of view that wasn't his, and carried it forward into his own life thinking he was a failure with money—and that's exactly what he created. He even had a girlfriend who kept telling him he was a failure with money. When he become aware that his father's money issue wasn't his and he started to use the clearing statement, everything in his financial universe began to change dramatically. And once he left the girlfriend who was convinced he was a failure with money, Dain started making money with ease. He made more money in the next three months than he had in three years.

People adopt viewpoints that aren't theirs all the time. Have you tried and failed—to handle your family's money issue or some other problem? Have you assumed it must be your problem? Have you adopted it as your problem so you have something to solve—because you are a good problem solver? You couldn't solve this problem because it wasn't yours to begin with. It still isn't your problem. It will never be your problem. But you have evidentiary contrivances that make it your problem. How many evidentiary contrivances and DJCCs do you have to make "your" problem—the problem that you don't have, that is actually somebody else's problem—into a problem you are trying to solve?

Have you been trying to handle your family's money issue since you were a kid? At what age did you start to handle your family's money issues? Everything you did to create the evidentiary contrivances and DJCCs of that, will you destroy and uncreate all of it? Right and Wrong, Good and Bad, POD, POC, All Nine, Shorts, Boys and Beyonds.

Who Does This Belong To? Not only do we take on other people's issues; we also take on their thoughts, feelings, and emotions, and we misidentify them as our own. In fact, 98 percent of "your" thoughts, feelings, and emotions do not belong to you. They belong to everyone else around you. You're a giant psychic radio receiver.

Dain says that one day he was sitting at the breakfast table before he was going to do a teleconference. All of a sudden, he started to feel frantic. He started looking for the email that had the teleconference number and the other information he needed to make the call. He was getting more and more worked up. "Where are they? Where are they?" All of a sudden, he stopped and said, "Wow, this is not like me. I don't get frantic like this. Okay, who does this belong to?" Instantly the frantic feeling lightened up and went away. It wasn't his.

Every time you feel yourself going into an emotion, thought, or feeling, ask, "Who does this belong to?" If it's not yours, it will immediately lighten up. It could belong to your neighbor down the street or to somebody walking by your apartment. You don't have to know who it belongs to; just return it to sender.

Use this tool every time you notice you have a limited point of view about money: "There's not enough money," "It's tough to make enough money," "I'll never have the right job," or any of the other crazy, limited thoughts you have about money. Some people get more benefit from asking the question three times. "Who does this belong to? Who does this belong to? Who does this belong to?" You can also ask, "Is this mine or someone else's?" If it lightens up at all, it's not yours. If it feels heavy, ask, "How did I create it?" or "Did I buy this as mine when it wasn't?" If that's the case, use the clearing statement.

Dain tells a story that is a great example of this. He said, "I had a good friend who gave me something as a gift, and for a split second after he gave it to me, I had the thought, 'He's giving me this so he can control me. He's going to use it against me later.'" I sat there with the lovely gift he had given me, and I felt really heavy.

"Then I suddenly remembered that whenever something makes you feel heavier, it's a lie. The truth will always make you feel lighter. I said, 'Wait a minute! Who does this belong to?' and it lightened up immediately. I used the clearing statement and it got even lighter.

"It wasn't until three months later that I suddenly realized, 'Oh! I bought that from my dad.' My father is a jealous person who always thinks people are out to get him. I had bought that viewpoint from him such a long time ago and had it in my world for such a long time that it seemed like it was mine."

From the moment you come in, you, as a being, are highly aware. You start looking around and thinking, "Hey, this place seems pretty cool. I'm going to see how it works." You check everything out. You check out the people and you perceive and receive everything that goes on with everyone. And because you're around your parents the most, you end up picking up the thoughts, feelings, emotions, and no-sex point of view that they have, and you end up buying those points of view as your own.

When we refer to a no-sex point of view, we are not talking about copulation, which is what most people think sex refers to. From an Access point of view, sex is the way you feel on those days when everything is going well, and you're feeling great. There's a certain energy that goes with this. You know you're looking good, everybody else knows you're looking good, and you're strutting your stuff. Have you noticed on these days, how much more you're willing to receive from everyone around you? Well, no-sex is the exact opposite of that. Another way of saying no-sex is no-receiving.

Even though you have decided you don't want to become your parents, have you noticed that you're creating a financial situation very similar to theirs? Do you know why that is? It's because as a kid, long before you even understood money, you bought their thoughts, feelings, emotions, and no-sex (no-receiving) point of view, and you've been functioning from them ever since.

> For the next week, every time you have a point of view about money, ask, "Who does this belong to?" You can also ask, "Is this mine or someone else's?" If it lightens up, return it to sender. If it gets heavier or it lightens up and then gets heavier, ask, "How did I create this?" or "Did I buy it as mine when it wasn't?" Everything that is, will you destroy and uncreate it and return it to sender with consciousness attached? Right and Wrong, Good and Bad, POD, POC, All Nine, Shorts, Boys and Beyonds.

When you use these questions, you'll start seeing things differently in your life. You will begin to notice the places where you have a limited point of view about money, and you'll see the places where you have an expansive point of view. You will begin to develop a different way of looking at the world, and because your point of view generates your reality, you will start to generate something totally different in your life.

The Four Elements
of Generating Wealth

There are four elements of generating wealth:

1. Be willing to have money
2. Generate money—don't try to create it
3. Educate yourself about money and finance
4. Generosity of spirit

To truly have consciousness with money and generate wealth, you have to be willing to have money, you have to be able to generate money, you have to educate yourself about money, and you have to incorporate a generosity of spirit into your life. These four things will make it possible for you to have the wealth you would like to have. We talk about each of these elements in the pages that follow, and offer lots of questions and other tools you can use to begin generating wealth in your life.

Chapter 4

The First Element of Generating Wealth

Be Willing to Have Money

Having Money vs. Getting Money, Saving Money, and Spending Money

Do you love to save money? I like to save. My ex-wife liked to save money, too. She'd come home and say, "Honey, I saved us $2,000 today."

I'd say, "Really? How did you do that?"

She'd say, "I bought a dress for $800 that was marked down from $2,800."

Like my ex-wife, a lot of people misidentify and misapply the idea of saving. They think saving means buying something on sale. Sorry, but that's spending. How about looking at the money you spent? Our friend Simone used to work in retail. She said that when they wanted to sell an $80 item, they would write $350 on a tag, draw a line through the $350, write $250, draw a line through it, write $150, draw a line through it, and then write $80. People would walk in the shop, look at the tag, and say, "Wow, look at this $350 jacket for $80! I'm going to buy it." They "saved" $270.

Having money is different from getting money, saving money, or spending money. Having money is a way of being in the world. It is a level of energy that feels like there is no lack in your life. There is the sense of having a choice. You don't feel like you need to get money. Getting money always comes from a sense of lack. "I can't afford this. I need this. I can't get this. I can't have this." Anytime you are thinking about getting money, you are focused on "not enough." You are functioning from the idea that you don't have enough—so you've got to get more.

Having money means you are not functioning from a sense of shortage. When you are willing to have money, you are able to generate it with no particular effort. We have a friend who is a great example of this. She came from a wealthy family, and she never had the point of view that she couldn't have money. In fact, she was completely willing to have money. She has always had plenty of money in her life. She gets jobs that pay her better than anyone else. She married a guy who was very wealthy, and today she still has plenty of money. Why is this? Because she doesn't have any points of view about not having money. To the contrary, she can have money.

Have you ever noticed that people with money always seem to get more money? Why is that? Because people like our friend are willing to have money; they like money. They are vibrationally compatible with money and vibrationally appealing to money. Money goes to them. Money finds the things that appeal to it, and the thing that most appeals to money is your willingness to have it. If you aren't willing to have money, you won't get money. I continuously see people saying, "I want to spend money." They don't have the idea of having money.

Some people spend money all the time. They keep spending and spending, and guess what? They don't have any money! They have spent it all. When you like to spend money more than you like to have money, you aren't going to have any money. Chances are, if you spend all the time, you actually hate money. People who truly love money are willing to have it and spend it. Many of us grew up in the age of instant gratification, and we are instant gratification junkies. When we want something, we expect to have it now. There's nothing wrong with this in and of itself, but it makes it hard to have money.

Some people complain about having to save money. They say things like, "It feels like I'm a slave to saving money" or "Saving money is no fun." When I hear this, I always ask, "Well, what about when you are working hard to get the money to pay for everything you bought last month? Are you a slave then?" Yeah, you are. That's what credit cards are for. So you can buy what you want, when you want it, and pay for it later. Do you realize that you are paying for your life—later? The truth is, you have to have more money than you can spend before you can spend as much money as you want. Most of us are not yet at that place—but there's a way to get there. The first thing you need to do is to start tithing to the Church of You.

Tithe to the Church of You

If you want to change your financial condition, you have to become willing to have money. A very important action you need to take is to set aside enough savings so you can function in your life for six months without any income. This is one of your beginning targets. You want to be able to cover your expenses for six months without working. Put the money in the bank or in your mattress, or wherever you want to put it, but arrange your life so you have that amount of money available to you. Once you have that, you will stop worrying about the rent, the utilities, and your monthly expenses, and you will start to generate more in your life. When you don't have that, you tend to you focus on "I don't have enough money."

How do you set aside enough money to cover your expenses for six months? You do this by tithing to the Church of You. Set aside 10 percent of every dollar that comes in and put it into a savings account for you. Some people teach that you need to tithe 10 percent to your church, put 10 percent away for this, put 10 percent away for that, and then put 10 percent away for you. No. First you tithe to yourself. Tithing to the Church of You is an honoring of you. It's about thanking yourself for what you generate and create. Then you pay your bills. If you do this for six months, your whole financial situation will begin to turn around. The 10 percent begins to grow until it becomes such a large amount that you no longer think about money; you just keep generating it. People who don't have money put a great deal of attention on not having money. They say, "I've got to get money," but once you have money, you don't think about it anymore.

There's an amount of money you will accumulate by putting away your 10 percent—you may not know what it is—but once you reach it, all of your stress and attention on money will go away. For Dain, initially it was $50,000. When he had saved $50,000 from the 10 percent he was setting aside, he suddenly felt relaxed about money. Without even realizing it, he had decided, "Once I have $50,000, I will be okay." Everyone has an amount like this. The money you have tithed to the Church of You gives you an awareness of what it's like to have money. When you get to this point, whatever it is for you, your stress about money comes off, and you generate even more with great ease. It's about finding a new way of interacting energetically with money and your life, which creates entirely new possibilities for you.

A woman once said to me, "I get angry sometimes because I have to concentrate on money. Can't I just bypass the whole money thing and just receive what I need?"

I asked, "Can you get air without breathing?"

She said, "No."

I replied, "The same thing applies to money. Money is like air; it goes in, it goes out. When you breathe in air, part of it stays in your blood. But when money comes in, you get rid of it all. You never keep any of it in you. That's a mistake." You can lessen the attention you put on money by putting that 10 percent away. People who have money don't think about money, but they remember to breathe deeply of the money they have.

Save 10 percent of what you gross—not what you net. If you get $100, put $10 away, no matter what. This point is important, because you can always finagle with the gross and net so you're not putting away the full 10 percent. It's called creative accounting. Don't engage in creative accounting. Put away the full 10 percent of every dollar that comes in. The money that you tithe to the Church of You should not be invested in shares or anything with volatility. It should be in cash assets: dollars, gold, or silver—something that you can sell instantaneously. You want it to be liquid.

People ask us if they can spend the interest they earn on that money. I say, "Yeah, you can spend it if you're stupid." You can spend the interest if you wish to, but spending the interest doesn't demonstrate the willingness to have money. It is about spending money. If you're more focused on what you can spend than on what you can have, you will not generate massive amounts of money. The question is: Where do you want to be at the end of your life?

People also ask if they can use their 10 percent to buy something they want. The answer is no. That's the wrong way to think about it. Rather than spending what you have saved, you need to ask, "What else can I add to my life?" Otherwise you're stuck in that old point of view of, "All I've got is this."

A man in one of our classes said to me, "If I decide that I need to set aside 10 percent a month like you said, and then I see something that I want and I don't have the money for it, what should I do? For example, say I want to take an Access Success course. What is more important for me? This 10 percent is an abstract thing. I don't know what it means. But the course can be beneficial for me—or fun—so, what do I do? It's hard for me to make sense of this."

I told him, "The 10 percent is about honoring yourself first. Don't spend your 10 percent on Access classes. Instead ask, 'What can I add to my life to create more money so I can pay for this Access class?'" You want to add to your life so you generate more money, not subtract from the account that you set up to honor yourself. You aren't going to get more by subtracting from something you have.

Set Aside 10 Percent of What Comes Into Your Business

If you have a business, we recommend that you also set aside 10 percent of everything that comes into your business. Even if your business is in the red and you have to pay debts to overcome that red ink—and it seems totally impossible to put away 10 percent— do it anyway. I've been there. My business was in the red, and I started putting away 10 percent of every dollar that came in. I borrowed money to keep the business going, but I took 10 percent of the money I borrowed and put that into the savings account. And in about six months, everything started to turn around. Why did this work? Get the energy of "my business is in the red." Now get the energy of "I have x number of dollars in my business savings account." Which energy is more generative?

When I started out, if I needed $10,000 to keep my business going, I would borrow $8,000 and try to earn the rest. That didn't create the right energy. Finally I got smart and borrowed $50,000. That turned the business around. I had a schedule to pay it off over five years, and I offered the lenders a higher interest rate than they could get anywhere else, so I made sure that my loan was always the first bill I paid—after I set aside the 10 percent, of course!

Carry Money in Your Pocket

In addition to tithing to the Church of You, you need to carry plenty of money in your pocket. When you carry money around with you and don't spend it, it makes you feel wealthy. You feel like you have money. More and more money can then show up in your life because you are telling the universe that you are abundant.

Decide upon a sum of money that you, as a rich person, will always carry with you. Whatever that amount is—$500, $1,000, $1,500— carry it in your wallet at all times. We don't mean carry a gold credit card. That doesn't cut it. Plastic is not cash. You've got to carry cash in your pocket, because it's about recognizing the wealth of you.

I carry two gold coins with me all the time. They're worth $843 each, so I always have $1,686 in my pocket. I always know I have money. Some people don't like to carry money with them because they worry about getting robbed. I tell them, "When you aren't paying attention, you could get robbed. But if you're carrying a sizeable amount of money with you, you'll be more aware of what's going on around you, and you won't get robbed." If you always carry cash, you can't afford the stupidity of unconsciousness, which is what allows you to be mugged. You'll always be aware. You'll say, "I've got stuff here that's worth a lot."

A woman once said to me, "I went on a trip, but I didn't bring my real jewels because I was staying in a bad section of town, and I didn't want to take the chance of getting ripped off." I said, "Honey, when you're in a bad section of town, go ahead and wear your real jewels. Everybody will think they're fake, because no fool would wear real stuff." Of course when you do this, you also have to be willing to be the energy of the killer—not the energy of the victim. You will be a victim to those who would kill if you're not willing to have the energy of killer. Do you want to be the effect of life, or the generator of life?

Eliminate These Words from Your Vocabulary

When people are used to having money, they have a different concept of life. There is no sense of lack in their world. The energy of having is part of their life. Their point of view is, "Oh well, I'll get that, one way or another." That's what life is like for them. There is plenty of money. Their point of view is, "That's the way life is." They continue to generate money just because they've always had it.

People who don't have money have a totally different energy in their lives that is based around a sense of lack, and they use words that express their sense of not having enough. If you'd like to become rich, there are six words we suggest you eliminate from your vocabulary: why, try, need, want, but, and never.

We often hear people say, "I'm going to try to do this. I'm going to try to do that." Does that lead to doing? Usually not. Say, "I'm going to try to stand up." Did anything happen or is your butt still firmly planted in your chair? It's probably still firmly planted because the word try means to attempt without ever succeeding.

Are you trying to handle your financial situation without ever succeeding? Everything that is, will you destroy and uncreate it and return it to sender with consciousness attached? Right and Wrong, Good and Bad, POD, POC, All Nine, Shorts, Boys and Beyonds.

Another word that's important to eliminate from your vocabulary is want. People who have money never use the word want. The word want has twenty-seven different definitions, all of which mean "to lack." Only in modern times has it acquired the meaning to desire or to wish for, and even that is still looking for something in the future. Be aware that when you use the word want, whatever you say or think will show up in your life. When you say "I want more clients," you usually end up with fewer. When you say, "I want money," you're saying "I lack money," and that's what shows up in your life.

In our money classes, we ask people to say, "I don't want money" ten times, and then we ask them whether they feel lighter or heavier. Lighter refers to a sense of expansion and possibility and a greater sense of space. You might even smile or laugh out loud. Heavier refers to a feeling of contraction, of things being weighted down and heavy. There is a diminished sense of what's possible. The truth always makes you feel lighter. A lie always makes you feel heavier.

Try it. Say, "I don't want money" ten times.

> I don't want money.
> I don't want money.
> I don't want money.
> I don't want money.
> I don't want money.
> I don't want money.
> I don't want money.
> I don't want money.
> I don't want money.
> I don't want money.

What happens for you? Do you feel lighter or heavier?

A man in one of our classes learned this tool. The next day before he went to a band rehearsal, he said, "I don't want money" ten times. A couple of hours later, when he was in the rehearsal, a guy in the band walked up to him and said, "Man, I've owed you a hundred bucks for so long. I keep meaning to pay you back, and I keep forgetting to do it," and he handed him a check for $600.

Having money is not what you have to spend. It's not the debt you build up as a way of proving you have money. Having money is the willingness to have money just sitting there without a "purpose." You will know when you have become willing to have money—because having it will become more important than spending it. You don't live beyond your means. You enjoy and live comfortably with what you have.

Too Much Money?

If you're going to have lots of money, something in your life has to change to accommodate that. Does that make sense? You've got to say, "I'm willing to have my life show up differently."

Dain says he used to spend his life in the "getting money" mode. He always had barely enough money. Then one day a very odd thing happened. There was more than enough to pay the bills. It felt very strange to him. He thought something must be wrong. What was "wrong" was the stress about money that he'd had all his life was suddenly gone. He had too much money. He had lived his entire life based on the idea that there was a certain amount that was required and that he could go above it a little bit or below it a little bit, and that would not cause stress. But when he went above it a lot, he went, "Aaargh!" He says, "I didn't know how to be me anymore. I didn't have any of the same parameters for being that I had when I didn't have more than enough money."

Fortunately he had done enough Access to know that he needed to ask a question. He said, "Wait a minute, what kind of a question is aaargh?" He asked, "What question could I ask that would allow me to see this situation clearly and to have a different point of view about it?" The question was, "Wow, what has changed for me that I haven't acknowledged?" Once he asked that question, he realized this was exactly what he'd been asking for since he started Access!

This often happens to people. They generate a whole lot of money and then they decide, "This can't be right. I shouldn't have gotten this money." A friend told us she was working with a client who overeats, and at one point the client said to her, "I eat to contract myself, because it's too uncomfortable for me to feel expanded." That's how it can be with money. "Too much" money makes you feel uncomfortably expanded. You're used to feeling contracted. This sort of thing often happens with people who win the lotto. Within five years, 98 percent of them are back in the same spot they were in before they won. Why? Because the stress they have about money and debt is what they consider their life. Anything else feels foreign, strange, and uncomfortable. They're not willing to be without the "not enough" feeling they consider normal.

How many evidentiary contrivances and DJCCs do you have to create the parameters of the amount of money you're willing to have—or not have? Everything that is, will you destroy and uncreate it all? Right and Wrong, Good and Bad, POD, POC, All Nine, Shorts, Boys and Beyonds.

What Energy Are You Refusing?

Some people refuse to be the energy of wealth by trying to control things with their judgments. When I first met Dain, he was working as a chiropractor in a tiny little office. He says, "That little office was the largest space I could afford, and it was also the largest thing that I could control with ease." Many of us do something like this. We choose to have the largest life that we know we can be in control of, which means we refuse the wild, abundant, out-of-control energy of the universe. Richard Branson has about 300 companies, including Virgin Records, Virgin Airlines, Virgin Mobile, and any other company that has the word Virgin in its name. Do you suppose he is in control of all that? No. He's willing to connect with his businesses and to direct them, but he doesn't try to control them. He would have to make his life and his business very small if he wanted to control everything.

I was working with a woman who had a lot of money. She was looking for a new house. One day as we were driving together, I saw a house and asked, "What about that house?"

She said, "Oh no, that's too big. If you have too much house or too much money, you can't control them."

I asked her, "Do you realize the limitation that viewpont is? Has your money grown in the last ten years?"

"No," she said, "it has diminished."

During the best years of our economy, her wealth had diminished. The amount of money she had did not grow because she was refusing to be the energy of a big house or lots of money. She thought that by refusing to have too much house or too much money she could be in control of what she had. Instead she was limiting what she could receive. When you're refusing to have too much house or too much money, do you have any choice? No. The only choice you are making is not to let your life expand.

People often put a stop on the energy of money coming into their life. They say, "Okay, I'm comfortable with the amount of money I'm making." What does that do? It stops additional money from coming in—and it stops the energy of all the things they want to create and generate.

If you are interested in clearing away the stops on the energy of money coming into your life, ask "What energy am I refusing that keeps me from having money?" The question brings up the energy you are refusing, and the clearing statement undoes it—which will allow money to show up. It's a slightly different point of view from psychological and metaphysical thinking, where the viewpoint is,

"If I can just see it, then I can change it." No. You've seen a lot of things that have never changed. Just ask the question and use the clearing statement. It's not just about awareness; it's also about allowing the energy to manifest. You ask the question to actually bring up the energy, and then you use the clearing statement to get rid of it.

What energy are you refusing that keeps you from receiving money? Everything that is, will you destroy and uncreate it all? Right and Wrong, Good and Bad, POD, POC, All Nine, Shorts, Boys and Beyonds.

Be Willing to Perceive, Know, Be, or Receive Everything

As we've said, if you wish to be truly abundant and to have everything—including outrageous amounts of money—you have to be willing to receive everything. You also have to be willing to perceive, know, and be everything in life. Anything else is functioning from judgment, which cuts off your ability to be, do, have, and receive everything.

When I was in real estate, I had clients who would say, "I want a fixer upper." I'd take them out and show them fixer-upper houses. They would hate those houses. Then I'd take them to a house that just needed some paint and new carpeting, and they would fixate on the fact that the carpeting was old and ugly. They couldn't see anything else in the house except the carpeting.

I'd say, "What about the structure? Look at the nice, high ceilings and the big rooms. Look at those great windows."

They would say, "What structure?" They couldn't see it.

I would point out that this house was everything they had asked for. They couldn't see that. All they could see was the ugly carpet.

That's what we do with our lives. Because of our judgments, we refuse to perceive, know, be, or receive the infinite possibilities that are available. We don't see the great fixer uppers in our lives. All we can see is the orange shag carpeting. When there is something you're refusing to perceive, know, be, or receive, how much effort do you have to use to keep that energy out of your life? Megatons! It takes a huge amount of energy to keep all your judgments in existence. But when you let go of those judgments, then all the energy of the universe, including the energy of money, is accessible to you.

What are you refusing to perceive, know, be, or receive that is keeping you from being, doing, or having what you would like to have in your life? Everything that is, will you destroy and uncreate it all? Right and Wrong, Good and Bad, POD, POC, All Nine, Shorts, Boys and Beyonds.

Chapter 5
The Second Element of Generating Wealth
GENERATE MONEY

Generation vs. Creation

We are taught that matter, space, energy, and time are the elements we need to create anything in this reality. When we function from the point of view of this reality, we use matter, space, energy, and time to create. If you're building a house you assume that you need a space to create in, which is the lot. You assume it's going to take time. You assume you need the matter called building materials. And you assume that it's going to take a certain number of man hours, called energy. These are the elements of the creation cycle.

The cycle of creation requires the continuous input of energy into a creation. If you don't, it eventually falls apart. It results in destruction. So, once you have a house, you need to continuously maintain it. You have to paint it regularly, you have to repair the roof, and you have to mow the lawn; otherwise, everything begins to disintegrate. And who is it that has to put that energy in? That's you.

Generation is different from creation. Generation is an energy that continuously brings things into existence. Have you ever had one of those moments when you thought about something and it came into existence instantaneously? Or you were looking for something and it immediately showed up? Or you thought about somebody and they called at that moment? These experiences are different from creation. They're generation.

We encourage you to look at how to generate more money in your life rather than how to create more money or make more money. In order to create, you have to work. You have to use matter, energy, space, and time. But when you generate something, you contribute to what is already in existence. Rather than fighting what's already here, use it and go with what will generate more. This world is already created the way it is. Why would you try to reinvent it? Generating is so much easier than trying to pound something into existence. Anytime you are functioning in contextual reality, you are creating, not generating.

Unlike the scientific construct on which this reality is based—the idea that everything is created from matter, energy, space, and time—the elements of generation are energy, space, consciousness, and the prima materia. The prima materia is the primary building source for what created the universe. It doesn't involve a molecule; it's the consciousness that we are. If we are the consciousness involved, and we use the energy, the space, and the consciousness to generate our lives, then our lives become expansive and joyful. We don't have the idea that we need to destroy what we have in order to create something different.

What this means is that energy, space, and consciousness are the source for generating anything we wish to have in our life. We don't have to create money from effort. In order to generate money, we just have to do things differently. Do you think you have to work hard for your money? Money is easy, but everybody says it has to be hard, and you go into agreement with them and try to make it hard to have money.

Dain and I would like to assist you to increase your ability to generate—not your ability to create. You already know how to create things. So how do you get to the energy, space, and consciousness that generate your life? In this section, we'll give you some tools you can use to generate the life that you would like to have.

Generating Your Life

There was a point in my life where I felt I'd done everything in life. I said, "I've had the house, I've had the car, I've had it all and lost it all. I've filed every form of bankruptcy known to mankind. I've been through it all." I understood what bankruptcy was, and I understood that it was a choice I had made. I thought, "Okay, so what am I going to do now?" I had no clue what I wanted. I knew what my wife wanted, I knew what my children wanted, and I knew what my friends wanted. I put all that aside and asked myself, "What do I want?"

The problem for most of us is that we're psychic beyond our wildest dreams, and we always know what everybody else requires and desires as their life. The difficulty comes when we misidentify and misapply what they require and desire—and believe that must be what we require and desire as well. Asking questions is the best way around this.

In my case, I asked, "What would I like my life to look like?"

I answered, "Well, I'd like to travel at least two weeks out of every month. I'd like to make at least $100,000 a year. I'd like to work with interesting people. I'd like to do something that would actually change the world. I'd like to do something that never bored me. I'd like to continuously expand some part of my life and everybody else's." That was the sum total of what I came up with as the answer to what I wanted to create as my life.

I got the energy or the feeling of what it would be like to have all those things as my life. I put that energy out in front of myself, and I pulled energy into it from all over the universe. Then I let little trickles of that energy go out to all the people who were looking for me and didn't yet know it. I did this about every three days so I could continue to be aware of what that energy felt like.

I noticed any opportunity that came into my life that felt like that energy, and I would do it, whether it made sense to me or not. One day I got a call from a guy in New York who wanted me to do a "guided massage." I had no idea what that was. It wasn't something I particularly wanted to do, but the energy of his request matched the energy of the six things I wanted as my life. So without understanding any more about it, I followed the energy. I flew to New York to work with the guy—and Access came into being out of that experience. Your energy, your space, and your consciousness of knowing what you want will lead you to what you're looking for. It goes beyond your mind, which only works within the limited construct of matter, energy, space, and time.

This is the way you can know what to choose in your life without trying to figure out the next step. You bypass the limited answers your mind provides, and you allow the universe to let you know what the next step is. It's a totally different way of generating your life. I let the six things that came up when I asked myself, "What would I like my life to look like?" determine the way my life should be.

You have to define what you would like to have as your life. Ask, "What do I want to do with my life? What do I want to do in my life?" If you don't have an answer to these questions, you end up in a nebulous place where the universe can't contribute to you. You don't know where to put the energy to generate your life. You don't know what to choose. Everything you choose in your life should be based on the energy you'd like your life to be. If you don't have a clue about what you'd like your life to be, you have no idea what to choose or where to go, which is one of the reasons you choose what everyone else needs, wants, and desires instead of what you desire. If something presents itself to you, you don't know whether it matches the energy of what you'd like to have as your life because you have no idea what you'd like the energy of your life to be.

It's not "I want a red BMW convertible and an estate on the French Riviera." That's not what you're looking for here. What you're looking for are all of the elements that you would like to have in your life and the energy they would be in your life. This is not about defining your life in terms of the car, the house, or the family you would like to have. These things show up as part of your life—they aren't the source of your life. We know too many people who have made their children the source of their life, but then their children leave home to create their own lives, and the parents end up seeing them twice a year, or the kids end up disliking their parents and not having anything to do with them. That's your life? No. It's not about the stuff you own or the things you have. It's not where you live. It's not what you do or the kids you have. It is the energy, space, and consciousness you're willing to be.

Notice that we're talking about the energy you'd like your life to be. We haven't mentioned money. Why is that? If you are willing to have and be the energy of what you'd like to have your life be, you will generate the money to make it show up.

What would it take for you to be willing to live the energy of what you would like your life to be so that it could show up for you in totality? Everything that doesn't allow that and all the thoughts, feelings, emotions, and no-sex that you're using to absolutely refuse and reject your life and the energy you would like your life to be, will you destroy and uncreate it please? Right and Wrong, Good and Bad, POD, POC, All Nine, Shorts, Boys and Beyonds. Do this thirty times a day for thirty days—and see what happens in your life.

Consider for a moment what it would be like if there were no limitations. Ask. "If there were no limitations—if I could choose anything—what would I choose as my life? If matter, energy, space, and time were not the criteria for my choice, what would I like to make as my life?" If there were no limitations on time, money, or ability, what would you choose? If you could do what you truly loved to do, what would you choose? What kind of people would you like to work with? What starting income would you like to have? What kind of impact would you like to have on the world? What emotional or energetic feeling would you like your life to have? There's no right or wrong here. You don't have to choose what I chose. What would you choose if it were truly about your life? (And it is!) What would be expansive to you?

If there were no limitations on time, money, or ability—if you could choose anything—what would you choose as your life?

_____

_____

_____

_____

_____

_____

_____

If there were no limitations, and you could do what you truly loved to do, what would you choose?

_____

_____

_____

_____

_____

What kind of people would you like to work with?

_____

_____

_____

_____

What starting income would you like to have?

_____

_____

_____

_____

What kind of impact would you like to have on the world?

_____

_____

_____

_____

_____

_____

_____

What emotion or energetic feeling would you like your life to have?

_____

_____

_____

_____

_____

Now that you have defined the energy you wish to have as your life, do the following four steps:

Get the energy or the feeling of what it would be like to have all the things you want as your life. At this point you probably won't have a clue about how this is going to happen. It's always going to look different from the way you think it's going to look. That's why it's important not to try to think it through. Just get the energy of the way it would feel to have all the elements you would like to have in your life.

Once you have the energy of what it would feel like to have all those elements in your life, put that energy out in front of yourself. It may be helpful to see it as a big energy ball. Now pull energy into it from all over the universe. Notice how your heart opens up when you do this. Continue to pull energy into that ball. You are pulling energy from the entire universe; you're connecting it to the entire universe. Continue to do this every three days so you continue to be aware of what the energy you desire feels like.

Now let little trickles of that energy go out to all the people who are looking for you and to everyone and everything that is going to help make it a reality for you. You don't have to know who they are or where they are. Just let the energy move out into the universe to reach those people.

Notice any opportunity that comes into your life that feels like that energy, and do it, whether it makes sense to you or not. The energy, your space, and your consciousness of knowing what you want will lead you to what you're looking for.

Follow the Energy. Following the energy is totally different from using your mind to figure things out in a linear way. When you're using your mind to figure things out, you are making lists of advantages and disadvantages and asking yourself, "Where is the greatest benefit? Where will I win? Where will I lose?" and you're choosing the thing that seems to offer the greatest win. That way of making choices has nothing to do with seeing energy in terms of what it will generate in your life.

When you use the linear method of figuring out advantages and disadvantages, how does it feel for you? We're guessing that it probably feels heavy to you. That's because in order to use the linear method, you have to go into a place of judgment and either/or. You can do this—or you can do that. There's no other choice. There are no other possibilities. No one has ever told you there is an approach to making choices that allows you to stride through life on seven league boots, which allow you to travel five, ten, or fifty miles with each step you take.

How do you follow the energy? Let's say you have several opportunities to choose from—A, B, and C. Get the energetic result or the feeling that each alternative will create in your life—and then choose the one that feels most like the energy in the energy ball exercise. What energetic result will occur with each alternative in the next six months, the next year, and in the next two years? Which alternative produces the most expansive energy and the greatest sense of possibility? Which has the lightest and most joyful energy? Which one matches the energy of the life you wish to have? Go with that one.

This is living your life from the energy of it. This energy is something you can be aware of, it's something you can talk to, it's something you can manipulate and change. Most people don't have any idea of what their life is—or what they want it to be. But when you start looking at your life as an energy, you begin to have a greater awareness of possibilities, ways to be, directions you can take, and things you can generate.

Doing Something You Don't Believe In. When you do something that you don't believe in, you will do yourself in with it. If you don't believe what you're doing is valuable, good, or right for you, you will always lose money or become less-than in some way as a result. Years ago, I used to sell pot. I thought it was cool. One day after a period of time, I saw I was in debt for the exact amount of money I had made selling pot. I realized that I saw selling pot as a way of making money without having to work, but I didn't really believe that it was a good idea. I decided that I needed to change my life because I was doing a lot of drugs, sex, and rock-and-roll, but that had not created a life of happiness. Like me, a lot of people make the decision to do things they don't believe are valuable or right for them because they think they will make money without working. This is not about being ethical. And it's not about judging what's right or wrong. It's about being aware of what works for you.

Be proud. People often believe that nothing they do has an effect on the world. If you have that point of view, you won't be able to change your financial situation or your life. You are refusing to be proud of everything you are, everything you do, and everything you have. And if you have no pride in what you are, then nothing you have or do is of any value.

If you do artwork and you are not proud of your work, you will diminish it and put it in the closet. You won't show other people what you've done. But you can't possibly be a success if you never let anyone see your art! You have to be willing to let people see what you've done and let them have their own point of view about it. You have to have pride in what you do. If you don't, you'll never succeed at it. You will diminish what you're doing and make it worth nothing. It's not that pride goeth before a fall, it's that without pride, you can't fall—but you also can't get anywhere.

What do you love to do? What do you love to do that you don't think you can get paid for? There is something that you have as a talent and ability that is so easy for you that you assume you couldn't possibly get paid for doing it. You think, "Nobody would pay me for doing that! It's so easy for me that everybody must be able to do it." You ignore and refuse the ability that will make you the most money. You've been taught that which is hard to achieve is valuable, so you discount anything that comes easily and naturally to you.

Years ago when I was in the upholstery business, I noticed I had a talent for seeing colors clearly and remembering them exactly. I would be working with someone who had an Oriental rug, and they would point to a color in the rug and say, "I want a chair that color." Weeks or months later, I would be in a fabric store and I would see fabric the exact color the person wanted. I would call them and ask if they had found their chair yet, and whether they would like me to buy them that fabric to upholster a chair. They would say, "Oh, yes, please buy the fabric!" I'd get the fabric and sell it to them for the exact amount I paid for it. What ability did I have that I wasn't valuing? My ability to see what others could not see. It came so easily to me I never considered it might be something people would pay me to do.

You have to ask yourself, "What do I love to do, that I assume no one would ever pay me for?" You have to do what you love. What do you love to do most? You may have no idea what it is because you discounted it years ago.

What do you love to do?

_____

_____

_____

_____

_____

What's really easy for you to do?

_____

_____

_____

_____

What's so easy for you to do that you think it must have no value?

_____

_____

_____

_____

What talent or ability do you have that you don't value because "anybody can do it"? (This may be the thing that will make you the most amount of money!)

_____

_____

_____

_____

Here is a process you might want to run, thirty times a day for thirty days or 100,000 days:

What generative energy, space, and consciousness can I be that would allow me to perceive, know, be, and receive the infinite contribution I truly be? Once you start to ask this question, you'll begin to see that you have an energy that you can contribute to things in a different way than you may have thought.

Celebrate Your Life. Hedonism is the willingness to seek the joy and the pleasure in every moment of life. When you walk outside and it's raining do you say, "Damn, it's raining!" or do you say, "Wow! Look at the rain!" When it's a really hot day, do you say, "It's frigging hot!" or do you say, "Wow, it's an amazingly hot day!" Hedonism is taking pleasure in everything. It's the joy in being alive. Do the birds stop singing, because it's a cloudy day? No. They sing no matter what. And does the fruit tree say, "I'm not going to have fruit this year, because I'm having a bad hair day?" No, those things give joyously all the time.

You have to be willing to see what kind of fun you can have with your life. Ask, "What could I add to my life that would make it totally fun for me?" It's not about more free time. This is not what you need. It's something that makes your life fun. It's not extreme sports. It's about celebrating your life.

Birgitta, a friend of ours who loves to surround herself with fresh-cut flowers, told us that someone said to her, "Wow, you spend a lot of money on flowers, don't you?"

Birgitta had never thought about it that way before, and she answered, "Yes, I really like them."

The person then asked her, "Why don't you buy plastic flowers? They look the same all the time, and they're less trouble. You would save a lot of money."

Birgitta didn't see it that way. She said, "I enjoy surrounding myself with nice, fresh flowers. I love the way they look and smell." Birgitta's life is about doing what feels right for her. She is celebrating her life. This is something you can do as well. You can make your life a celebration.

When I got divorced, I got one out of four sets of china and one out of four sets of sterling silver flatware. I got two cups, a few family heirlooms, and all the excess furniture that was in the basement. All of that, plus $100,000 worth of debt. That's what I took out of the marriage. My ex-wife got a half million dollars' worth of antiques, a half million dollars in jewelry, no debt, and a bunch of money from me.

I moved out of our house into an apartment. I put the china away in a high cupboard, thinking, "I'll save this for a special occasion." Since I didn't have any junk silverware, I put the sterling silver in the drawer and started to use it. And then, looking up at the china in the cupboard, I thought, "Wait a minute. I'm old enough that it's a special occasion when I wake up in the morning." I decided to use the china every day.

Celebration does not mean you spend money unnecessarily. Celebration is about the approach you take to your life. Life should be a celebration. It should be a joyful experience every day. Today I use good sterling, good china, crystal glasses, and all the best stuff. I figure if I'm alive today, that's a cause for celebration.

A lot of us put off celebrating our lives in all the ways we could. We think it has to be a special occasion before we buy flowers, drink champagne, or use the good china. A number of years ago, our friend Mary, who was 95 years old at the time, was living with us. Christmas was coming, and I asked, "Mary, what would you like for Christmas?"

She said, "I'd like some 600-count sateen sheets. That's what I'd like!"

Christmas Day came, and she opened her gift. She was delighted: "Lovely, new sheets! These are wonderful! I'll put them away for a special occasion."

I said, "Mary, if you wake up in the morning, it's a special occasion. And I don't see any men sneaking in here to visit your bed. So don't be saving those sheets! You should be using them and enjoying them!"

How much of your life, how many evidentiary contrivances and DJCCs do you have that keep your life from being a celebration? Everything that is, will you destroy and uncreate it all? Right and Wrong, Good and Bad, POD, POC, All Nine, Shorts, Boys and Beyonds.

Getting What You Desire. A lady told us she wished to move to Paris, where the company she worked for had a branch office. She asked, "How can I make that happen?"

I said, "Pull energy into it."

She asked, "How do I do that?"

I answered, "The same way you do when you flirt. You just pull energy." People often have trouble with this idea. Why do we think we don't know what it means to pull energy? Do you have a dog? Does it ever make you go to the door to let it out? It's pulling the energy. Do you always know when your cat is outside the door, waiting for you to let it in? It's pulling energy. Can you make someone who is giving a presentation call on you without raising your hand so you can ask a question? You're pulling the energy.

She said, "Okay! Can I start now, or do I need to go to Paris?"

I said, "Start right now. Keep pulling energy from everybody in your company that could make that happen until they can't not notice you."

It's totally natural to pull energy, especially if you want something. Have you ever decided that you wanted someone, and you just sat back and said, "Oh, baby, you're mine"? Children do this very well. If you've forgotten and you want to learn how to do this again, go to a playground and watch kids. Look for the one that reminds you of yourself. Watch that child pull energy. When you pull energy, you can create champagne bubbles in people's universe. Ask your body to keep pulling energy even when you're doing something else. This is the way to get what you desire.

Generating Money in Your Life

To generate the kind of money you would like to have in your life, you have to enjoy what you do. We see people getting involved in something because they decide it can make them some money or they decide, "This will work." Where is the question in that? There is none.

The approach should be, "Okay, I like to do this. Can I make money with it? Good. How much money can I make? Is there a limit to what I can make with this job, this technique, or this system that I have?" If there's a limit, and there's no problem with there being a limit, then you have to ask, "What's the top end I can make with what I'm doing?" If that is sufficient money for you, there's no problem. If it is not sufficient, you have to ask, "What else could I be, do, have, create, or generate that would be fun for me, and make me more money?" Fun for me, and make me more money. That's the key.

We sometimes see people getting into something and starting to make some money and then they say, "Okay! I'm making money now." Where is the question in that? It's not a question. It's an answer: I'm making money. We don't often see people asking the question they should ask: "Will this make me all the money I would like to make?" If it's not going to make you all the money you would like to make, then you need to find out what you can add to your life that will bring you up to the amount you would like to have. You have to ask, "What else can I add to my life?"

In these economic times, many people are asking, "What can I cut back on in my life so I have fewer bills?" It's quite a popular approach when the economy is difficult, but it's moving in a destructive direction. It's about making your life less. The more positive point of view is, "What can I add to my life?" That question will move things in a generative direction. It's not about cutting off things that you like; it's about adding things that you enjoy and that will make you more money. There are plenty of ways to generate money that are actually fun. You have to be willing to know that it's possible, and then find them. Most people have the point of view that making money is drudgery or they think it is painful or that they don't know how to do it. Use some of the ideas, questions, and tools that follow to help you generate more money.

Are You Charging Enough? A lady in one of our classes told us, "When I was young I used to baby sit. I charged 50 cents an hour. One day I said to my mother, 'I think I'm worth 75 cents an hour.' My mother said, "'Oh no, don't raise your prices! If you raise your prices, nobody will hire you anymore.'"

How's that for some lousy parental advice about money? A lot of people buy into this idea. They undercharge for the service or product they're offering because they think nobody will hire them if they raise their prices. They don't value the work they do, the product they create, or the service they perform. What do you get when you do this? You get low-quality clients. And what do you get when you raise your prices? The worst-case scenario is that you'll get some more free time. The best-case scenario is you'll get more free time and better clients!

Over and over again people tell us that they have raised their rates, and they actually have more business now that they're charging more. One woman told us that when she raised her rates, one of her clients said, "I can't afford that." She said, "Okay, I can send you to somebody else." Suddenly the person decided she could afford to pay her rate after all.

Sometimes people use a sliding scale with their clients. They charge based on what they think the client can afford. I did this once. A lady I was working on said, "I'm retired and I don't have very much money. Could you give me a discount because I'm a retired person?" I gave her a discount. As she was leaving, I said, "Let me walk you to your car." She said, "No, no, no, I'm fine." The energy of it was strange, so I went out the back door and around to the front of the house just in time to see her as she got into her Rolls-Royce and drove away. Now if people don't want to pay what I charge, I offer to send them to somebody who is willing to take what they're willing to pay. I'm valuable to me, and my time is worth the rate I charge.

Dain says he's learned that if people are not willing to pay your rate, they're not going to be willing to receive the gift you share with them, which is why you're doing your work in the first place. You want to give a gift that they will receive. It's not about the money. He says, "When I started out, I was charging x amount per session. As time went on, I started raising my rates, and I discovered the more I charged, the more people would receive from the sessions I gave them. If I charged ten times more than when I began, people would receive ten times more."

The gift that you offer to people, which is the gift that you are, becomes more dynamic the more you charge. There's nobody else in the world that does what you do. There is no competition for you. There's no one like you in the entire world. Someone may do something that's similar to what you do, but there's no one like you. If somebody wants you, they want you, and whatever you charge only makes you more valuable to them. If you are charging a lot, people know you've got to be good at what you do. All you have to do is deliver a good product.

If you raise your rates, you may lose one or two people, but you will gain ten. If you have your own business or if you're doing a specialty thing that only you are doing, you have to charge an amount that makes you happy to do it. Don't work for cheap. It doesn't matter what you do. Never charge the going rate. It's not about what the traffic will bear; it's about the product you create for them and how much you are going to enjoy the money they give you. You have to know you're good at what you do. And the only way people are going to know you're good is if you charge a lot of money!

How many evidentiary contrivances and DJCCs do you have so that you never charge as much as you're worth, and you never charge people enough that they will actually desire to throw money at you and pay you? Everything that is, will you destroy and uncreate it all? Right and Wrong, Good and Bad, POD, POC, All Nine, Shorts, Boys and Beyonds.

Look for the Opportunities. Great amounts of money are not created from perspiration; they're generated from inspiration. We are in an economic slowdown right now, and this means that now is the time to look for the opportunities rather than the disasters. You have to be willing to take advantage of people who are stupid enough to kill their finances and give you an opportunity, and there is always somebody who is willing to do that.

Sometimes people need to get rid of things they can't afford to keep, and that's an opportunity you can take advantage of. They might need to get rid of a car because it is costing them too much money or because they want to buy something else. We know people who suddenly were able to buy great cars for very little money. Why? Because the former owners needed to get rid of them. They needed to get those cars out of their financial liability column so that they could buy something that would be an asset for them.

You assume that you have to be good, right, and kind, and take care of everybody. Are you willing to give up your Nurse Nancy uniform? Give up the necessity of making sure you treat everybody equally, fairly, and righteously. Recognize that opportunity comes from people who are willing to cut their own throats. Maybe they are selling something valuable for less than it is worth. Someone might say that's taking advantage of them, but giving them the money they require can actually be a benefit to them. If they need $100,000 for something that would normally sell for $500,000, and you're there to provide the $100,000, it's a gift to them. The item you're buying may be worth $500,000, but there's no way they are going to be able to sell it for that amount in the current climate. When you give them $100,000, you may be getting $400,000 off the value of the item, but you might also be helping them out dynamically. If all you're willing to look at is, "I'm taking advantage of them," you'll miss a great opportunity. And they will miss out on the $100,000 they need.

You have to give the person on the other side of the deal his or her choice. You can't make choices for them. I once went to a garage sale and noticed a bracelet marked $15. I picked it up and saw that it had "14 karat gold" stamped on it. I thought, "This can't be right. It must be at least $115." I asked the lady, "How much is this?"

She said, "It's $15. And it's 14 karat gold, too."

I said, "Okay, you want $15, here's $15."

She said, "Oh, I'm so glad somebody got this who can appreciate it."

I had it appraised; it was worth $900. The strange thing is there were five antique dealers at this event in front of me, and they didn't buy it. They figured for that kind of money, the bracelet had to be a fake.

The lady appreciated the fact that she had given a gift to me. She wasn't looking for money; if she had been looking for money she'd have taken the bracelet to a pawnshop or a place that would have paid gold value for it. She wasn't interested in that; she just wanted somebody to love what she was getting rid of. Now, you could assume it's wrong to take advantage of an opportunity like this. But is it?

A friend told me a parallel story. He was in a supermarket in Japan a few years ago and there was a nice bottle of Margaux wine, a French wine that sells for hundreds of dollars a bottle. It was marked $8. He went to the checkout and asked, "Are you sure this is right? It says $8."

The manager said, "Oh, it's 1996. It's an old one. You'd better have it for $4."

He suddenly had an opportunity that came from awareness. He was aware of Margaux wine and knew what it was worth. The manager's point of view was, "This is an old bottle of wine. Why the hell would I want this? It's not even made of rice. Only stupid people drink wine made out of grapes. They don't know the good stuff."

We assume we need to educate people about the things we know. Get over the idea that you need to educate people! That's the biggest mistake most of us make. If people haven't asked you a question, they don't want to know. Do you really want to offend somebody? Try to educate them about something they've already decided they're right about.

It's different when you're dealing with someone who has made a mistake in giving you change. It's one thing when you have somebody offer you something when they're happy with what they're getting, but when you know the person is making a mistake and will have to come up with that money out of their pocket, that's a different story.

I've had it happen where I've given a cashier a $20 dollar bill and he gave me change for a fifty. I said, "Excuse me, I think you got this wrong."

And he said, "No, you gave me a fifty."

I said, "No, I gave you a twenty."

And he said, "No, you gave me a fifty," and then he looked in the drawer and saw that he put a twenty in the fifty slot. He said, "Oh, thank you, thank you, thank you."

I was not trying to act as his protector; I was just being honest with what was going on. There is a difference between screwing people out of money and recognizing an opportunity or a good deal when it's in front of you.

People seem to want hard and fast rules about what to do and when to do it instead of following the energy and being aware. They ask, "What's the rule I need to follow to get more money?" Our answer is awareness. Is it going to make you feel lighter to take $100 from a cashier who makes $8 an hour, and who's going to have to pay it back? If you follow your awareness, you will know what to do. Ask yourself what's going to be generative for you in your own life. Awareness is the important thing. In economic times like these, awareness opens the door to opportunities. When you're aware, you'll know what course of action to take; you'll see what can be done; you'll see what opportunities are available.

Is now the time? Before you start to pursue the opportunities you become aware of, ask, "Is now the time to start you?" or "Is now the time to institute you?" or "Is now the time to put this into motion?" Deciding that "now is the time" doesn't necessarily mean that now is the right time, but if you ask a question, you can determine whether it is the right time. You'll have lots of ideas before it's time to start them. If you ask "Hey, universe, hey project, hey me and my infinite awareness, is now the time to start this project?" you won't begin a project when the underpinnings for it are not yet in place. Sometimes things in the universe have to be rearranged before a project or an idea or an invention is ready to take off. You need to find out if it's an appropriate time for you to start. We often hear stories about people who were ahead of their time. They had wonderful ideas, but the world wasn't ready for them. People say things like, "He was ahead of his time," or "This idea was ahead of its time." There are a lot of things like this that people attempted to put into place before their time, and those projects had to sit in waiting for a couple of centuries before the time was right for them to catch on and become successful. That's not what you want to happen to you. You don't want to put your efforts into something that won't be ready to happen for another twenty years. So ask, "Is now the time to start you?" If you get a no, then say, "Okay, let me know when it is the time." Write your idea down on a piece of paper and put it in a drawer or in a tickler file that says "look at me again in a month or two." Ask the project, because everything has consciousness, "When do I need to be reminded of you again?" Allow the things in your life to help you to generate money.

Twenty years ago, certain financial rules were in place. You knew that if you invested in x, it was likely to go up this amount; if you invested in y, it was likely to go up that amount. Right now everything is in flux. There is a massive change under way, and with change comes opportunity. With change also comes depression. Right now, from our perspective, we're going into a depression, which means over the next fifteen years there's not going to be much growth, but there will be a great deal of opportunity.

Your point of view can create a totally different possibility; the choices you make can create a huge difference in what shows up for you. In 1990, right before Iraq invaded Kuwait, Dain was in college and he worked on a car lot selling used Chevrolets. Then the first Gulf War started and the bottom dropped out of the car market. Everybody's sales at the car dealership went down dynamically— except one guy's. His sales doubled when everybody else's were down 50 percent. Interestingly, he hadn't been a top salesman. This was a guy who dressed like a used-car salesman. He had bad breath and a mustache that always had food in it.

After a month of seeing this guy's sales go up, Dain went to him and asked, "What is going on? How is it that your sales are going through the roof and everybody else's have dropped in half?"

The guy said, "Well, people still have to buy cars."

Dain realized that everyone had adopted the viewpoint, "It's a recession. It's a depression. The bottom has dropped out of the car market." But this salesman was willing to take a different point of view and that made all the difference. His point of view created his reality.

The question is: What point of view would you like to choose regarding what's coming up? Would you like to stick yourself with the point of view, "Everything is falling apart. I'm going to be depressed like everybody else. I'm not going to have any money" or would you like to choose the viewpoint that you are going to find opportunities to generate money? You can ask yourself, "How can I get by and survive until things get better?" or you can ask, "How can I thrive, regardless of what's going on?" It's your choice. You can choose to look at things from a different place to figure out how to generate the life you'd like to have.

During the Great Depression, there were people who made a lot of money. For example, a lot of money was made in the entertainment industry. Why was that? Because people still wanted to be entertained. They were willing to spend their hard-earned money on entertainment. A lot of businesses were created during the Great Depression, and many of them thrived and expanded. That's when five and dime stores became hot. People loved them because they could buy something for a nickel or a dime, which is what they had to spend.

We're not talking about surviving piss-poor in hard times; we're talking about thriving during hard times. That means that now is the time to look for the opportunities rather than the disasters.

Are you one of those people who were alive during the Great Depression and got a new body in the meantime—but you're still focused on surviving the Depression? Are you still in survival mode and being as financially depressed as you can be? Will you destroy and uncreate all of that? Right and Wrong, Good and Bad, POD, POC, All Nine, Shorts, Boys and Beyonds.

Asking Questions

As we've said, everything in the universe is conscious, and everything supports you. When you choose consciousness, you'll begin to realize that everything in the universe is conscious, and every molecule will support you in ways you never imagined. You access this support by asking questions. Because Dain and I live in the question, we consistently receive in ways we never thought were possible. People, money, and things show up for us in ways we never expect. They come from some place in the universe to be in our life. It's like, "How did you get here?" Here are some of the questions we use.

If I buy you, are you going to make me money? Have you ever decided that investing in a house or a stock was going to make you a lot of money? But did it? If you ask the investment or the house or whatever it is a question and listen to its answer, you will always know whether it will make money for you. Ask, "If I buy you, are you going to make me money?" If you get a yes, it will make you money.

Ask this question of anything you are thinking about buying. When you do this, you have to put your beliefs and desires aside so you can receive the answer that is coming to you from the thing you are considering purchasing. If you have a strong conviction that an object, let's say a suit, will make you money no matter what, you're not going to hear the suit's answer. You're not actually asking it, "If I buy you will you make me money?" But if you ask the suit and truly listen for its answer, it will tell you yes or no. Nothing lies—except you. Things do not lie. This means you can ask them questions, and they will give you the information you request.

If I'm thinking about buying a car, I can ask the car, "Will you make me money?" Do I expect it to directly make me money? Not necessarily. This does not always play out in a direct line. The energy of each thing you purchase contributes to the energy of the whole. The energy of the whole then generates the money you would like to have. The car may be the way I get someplace where I will make money.

Asking the question is not about trying to come to a conclusion about how the thing is going to make you money. It's the willingness to have the awareness about whether it's going to make you money. I use this question with everything I consider buying, including my horses, my antiques, my clothes, even my underwear. I don't buy underwear unless it says it will make me money. I'm not a stripper, so peeling off my underwear doesn't make me money—but I am willing to look at everything as contributing to my life. And the more you are willing to allow things to contribute to your life and to gift to you whatever energy they have available, the more you can receive—and the more money you can have.

If you'd like to have more money, we suggest you question everything in your life. Ask, "Will this thing in my life make me more money?" Go through your entire life. "Will this thing—whatever it is—bring me more money?" It might be a relationship, the chest of drawers in your room, your car, or all these things. "Will this make me more money?"

You also have to know what you can afford. If you want to buy a house that requires an $800,000 loan, you have to know whether you can come up with enough money to cover the mortgage, taxes, and insurance. You have to know how much money it costs you to live per month, so you can determine whether you can afford it. If you're going to get a loan on something, you need to make sure that you can afford it and that it's going to be easy for you to make the payments. If making payments on a nice house is going to stress you out to the nines, is it really worth it? You need to ask the house, "Will you make me money?" Even with the house you're going to live in, ask, "If I buy you, will you make me money?" If you're going to rent the house, ask, "Will you make me money?" Everything you're going to spend money on, ask, "Will you make me money?"

Will this be rewarding? An alternative to the question, "Will this make me money?" is "Will this be rewarding?" The other day I went out to do some errands with a woman who works for us. We saw a great dress in the window of an upscale store, and I had her go in and try it on. It looked great on her. I asked, "Will it be rewarding to buy this dress for her?" and the answer was yes, so I got her the dress. At the time, I didn't know how it would be rewarding. I had no idea what that was going to look like. As it turned out, after I got her the dress, which was initially difficult for her to receive, she stepped up to a whole new place of receiving in her universe—and she started to generate more business.

Most of us want to know what "rewarding" is going to look like before we act. We wonder, "Okay, so where am I going to be rewarded? How am I going be rewarded? How much money am I going to make?" The rewards can lead to more money, but they do not necessarily come in the form of money. They can come in many different ways and might include getting more conscious with money. Here are some additional questions you can use.

Do I need to buy you now? Let's say, for example, that you're in a bookstore. There are three books you'd like to have. One is a novel, one is a business book, and one is a book of erotica. You've asked the question, "If I buy you, will you make me money?" and all three of the books have said yes. You've only got $50 to your name, and if you buy all three of the books, you are going to be broke. What do you do in a situation like this? You ask, "Do I need to buy you now?"

Do you really want to own me? Someone asked me, "There is something I want to purchase because it would be fun to have, but when I asked it if it would make me money, it said no. I'd still like to have it; it would be fun. Should I go ahead and buy it?"

My answer was, "Nope."

But there is something you can do in a situation like this. Ask, "Do you really want to own me?" If the answer is yes, ask, "At what price would you make me money?" It will tell you, and you can make an offer on it. When I do this, 99 percent of the time people take my offer.

Recently Dain told me he wanted a rug for his room, and I said, "They've got a great Chinese Nickels rug at such-and-such a store." He went to look at it. The owner was asking $3,500, which he said was down from $5,000.

Dain asked the rug, "Will you make me money?" and it said no.

He wanted the rug, but when it said no, he said, "Okay, too bad."

He called me and said, "The rug said it wouldn't make me money so I'm not going to buy it, but it is so cool. It's the only rug I've seen that's the perfect size and the perfect color."

I said, "Ask it if there's a price at which it would make you money."

He asked it, "At $3,000, will you make me money?" The rug said no. Then he tried, "At $2,750, will you make me money?" Again it said no. Finally he asked, "Will you make me money if I buy you for $2,500?" It said yes.

Dain said to the owner, "I know you were kind enough to give me a special price because you know Gary, and I appreciate that, but all I'm willing to spend is $2,500."

The guy said, "I'll take it."

At $3,500 the rug wouldn't make him money. The answer was a flat, no, but when he got down to $2,500, everything opened up, and it felt really cool to have it for that amount.

When you actually talk to an item you are thinking of buying, you realize there is a communication coming from the rug or whatever the item may be. The rug knows what price the owner will sell it for. You don't. The rug's willing to be smarter than you are.

Tell me when I have to sell you to make money. When you're thinking about investing in stocks, gold, silver, or that sort of thing, you need to ask, "Will you make me money?" But once you make an investment like this, you have to be aware on a daily basis. Ask it, "Tell me when I have to sell you to make money on you." Otherwise you could end up holding it for way too long, and the value will go down.

We know a lady who had a guy invest for her. He was a friend of hers, and in the course of two and a half months, she made $70,000 from a $10,000 investment. At one point, she knew she needed to take her money out, but she didn't want to offend her friend because he had made her so much money. She held on to the investment even though she knew it was time to sell. During the next six months the value of her investment went from $70,000 to $7,500.

She had received the information, "Take your money out now," but she didn't do it. When you are making investments, you've got to be aware that there is a time frame. Be sure to ask your investments, "Tell me when to sell you to make me money."

If you are an investment advisor, you could play with this to see if it works on your clients' accounts. Ask, "Stock, tell me when it's time to sell you." Sell some of the stocks when you're told to do it, and don't sell some of the others. See which ones make you the most money. In the last year gold has gone up and down roughly $100 per month. If you asked the gold, "Tell me what day I need to sell you," and "What day do I need to buy you" and you did that, you could make a great deal of money.

It's like learning a new language. Play with it, and as you play, you'll get better at seeing the nuances and clearly knowing, "It said no" or, "It said yes." If you continuously work with these questions, eventually you'll become much better at choosing the right time to buy and sell.

Is there anything we can do with you to make you into more money? What would you like to become? The idea of having money is hard for some people to get. They see money that is not invested, and they think, "That money is losing value. I should be using it." They're not willing to have the money. They think they need to do something with it. If you're in a situation where you have money that you would like to invest in some way, there is something you can do. You can ask your money to help you make more money. Ask it, "Is there anything we can do with you to make you into more money? What would you like to become?" You can also ask something how much to sell it for.

What will you sell for? Do you actually own anything? No. Do you own your car? No. Why not? Because you go to work to pay for it, it doesn't go to work to pay for you. It owns you; you don't own it. You don't own your furniture, your house, or anything else because you're the one who works to pay for those things, take care of them, polish them, and clean them. You're the servant and the slave to your house and your stuff. There is nothing you own. You're the steward of everything. That's all you are. You're the caretaker. You have control over those things temporarily. You don't own them; you just have possession of them for the moment. It's important to get clear about this. You are paying for them and working hard to take care of them. It might be a good idea to see if they are providing anything for you. Many people, once they think about it, say, "I don't want to polish the silver and dust the furniture!"

I tell them, "So, ask it where it wants to go where people will like to polish it. Or hire someone who will take care of it. Or put it away in boxes. Buy furniture that doesn't need to be polished. Get some cool looking stainless steel furniture that you don't have to polish. Get gold furniture. You don't have to polish gold."

Some people enjoy taking care of their stuff. I don't usually enjoy hand-washing dishes, but I love hand-washing our china. I enjoy the interaction of the water, the soapsuds, my hands, and the dishes. When I interact with those things, it feels good, and it adds to my life. It gives me a sense of peace to wash things, so I enjoy taking care of them.

But if you don't enjoy taking care of something, ask it, "What will you sell for?" If you've got something on your hands that you bought without asking whether it would make you money, you can ask it, "Do you want to stay in my life or is there somebody else you would like to own?"

Then ask the item, "What will you sell for?"

When you're going to sell a house—or anything else—always ask it, "What price will you sell for?" I ask, "Will it be $350? $400? $425? $450? Okay, less than $450. Will it be $435? Okay, less than $435. $432? Okay!" That's the price you ask.

I knew some people who wanted to sell their ranch. They'd had it on the market forever at $12 million, and it hadn't sold.

Their realtor said, "We need to drop the price to $9 million."

I asked the ranch, "What do you want to sell for?"

It said, "$15 million."

Can you imagine the realtor's face when the people raised the price to $15 million?

The realtor said, "You can't do that!"

They said, "Yes we can; we're raising the price to $15 million."

Two weeks later they had a full price offer from some buyers who were looking for a ranch just like theirs. The buyers had decided the ranch they wanted would cost $15 million. They weren't looking in the $12 million price range. They wanted to pay $15 million.

Who do you want to own? Do you have your house on the market? Don't try to sell your house, instead ask your house to find its new owner—the person it wants to own.

Some friends of ours were looking for a new house because their current place wasn't big enough for them. One day they found a place to buy, which had a thirty-day escrow—but they hadn't yet put their house on the market.

They called me and asked, "What do we do?"

I said, "Ask your house to reach out and find the person that it wants to own. Then pull energy into the house from all over the universe and let little trickles go out to all the people who are looking for it and don't know it. Then go find a realtor."

Two hours later a realtor called them and asked, "Is there any chance your house is on the market?"

A few days later they had a full-price offer with a thirty-day closing. They smoothly moved from one house to the other. This is a great example of the way you can generate a different possibility when you're willing to ask questions and function from the energy of things.

When you have a house that wants to own somebody else, simply pull energy into it from all over the universe, then ask the energy you're pulling into it to trickle out to all the people who are looking for it and don't know it. Then ask the house to equalize the energy when the person it wants to own walks in the door. You pull energy in from all over the universe, the "right" person shows up, the house begins to flow that same amount of energy to the person, and the person says, "Oh, this is the house I've been looking for!" They recognize the energy they've been seeking is the energy they're receiving.

A lady told us she had a house in Florida that had been on the market for a year and a half. She learned about equalizing the energy when she was at an Access seminar in Seattle and immediately began doing it. The next day someone from New Hampshire, who wasn't even in the house, felt the energy. He called the lady's realtor and made an offer on the house.

Using Questions in Your Business

People tend to get their relationship going, or they get their business going, and then they try to keep it the same, thinking they're going to continue to get the same results they've been getting. But that's not how it works. You've got to be willing to change things at all times. Most businesses have a lifespan of seventy-five years, which is the expected lifetime of a human. Why is that? Because people get a good idea for a business, and they start creating from it. Then they decide they've got the right idea, and they don't change anything. They keep everything exactly the same. This is the same way we kill our bodies. If you decide that you have the "right" eating style and all the "right" habits, you stop dealing with your body in the moment. You make a decision about the way something is supposed to be, and you continue on with that decision. Your body might like being a vegetarian for two or three years and then it will say, "Okay, I've had enough of that. I want something different." That happened to me. I had been a vegetarian for three years, and one day I walked into a deli in New York, and my body screamed, "Steak! I want steak!"

I said, "Okay, fine," and I ordered a steak.

The waiter asked, "How do you want it done?"

I said, "Raw."

He said, "We can't do that."

I asked, "What's the least amount you can cook it?"

He answered, "One minute on each side."

I said, "Okay, then, that's how I want it."

It was the best-tasting thing I've ever had in my life. I had been vegetarian before, and when I went back to eating meat, my body threw up for three days. Not this time. The steak was exactly what my body wanted. I now listen to my body, and it tells me what it wants. I don't have the viewpoint, "I eat this—and I don't eat that."

The same thing applies to your business. If you decide, "This is the way we are doing business," you stagnate because you come out of the question. You stop doing what's new; you stop creating. You eventually devolve into death. This often happens in large companies. IBM, for example, used to be the big guy in the computer industry, and then all kinds of smaller companies that were more innovative came in and took huge parts of their market share. IBM went into a big decline. One day they finally said, "Hm, we've got a choice here: change or die." They brought in people to see what they could do differently. Now their corporate culture is completely different, and in every area where they've become innovative, they've started growing again. Today they function more like Google than like the big, old, conservative IBM.

What can I change that will generate more business today and tomorrow and every day after that? Asking questions with your business helps you to make the changes that will keep it vital and generative. A helpful question is, "What can I change that will generate more business today and tomorrow and every day after that?" Oftentimes what you change alters the business to make it more economically viable. And the answer is not necessarily downsizing, although it may be. We're not saying you shouldn't let anything go. You have to be willing to let anything go that needs to leave, whatever it happens to be—whether it's a relationship, employees, or stuff you have—so that everything is contributing to the life you'd like to have.

Sometimes it's appropriate to downsize, lay people off, or cut their salaries. If you're thinking about doing this, you can give them a choice. You can meet with them and say, "We're suffering in these economic times and we have a choice; we can either lay off a bunch of people or everyone can take a cut in salary. Do you have a preference? Would you rather be laid off or take a cut in salary?" It's amazing how many people will ask, "Well, can't we do something to generate more business?" Those are the ones you want to keep! If no one asks that question, you've probably got the wrong employees, which means that getting rid of them or cutting their salaries is the appropriate thing to do.

If I lay this person off, will it generate more money? This is a very useful question, because there are people who contribute to the energy of your business even though they don't seem to be doing a lot. And there are other people who seem to be doing a lot, but they're actually destroying your business. Ask, "Is this person generating more money for the business? Will keeping him generate more money and more business, or will getting rid of him generate more money and more business?" These are important questions because downsizing may be what you need to do in order to become more economically viable—but maybe it's not the right action.

Will this person make more money? Use questions when you're hiring people as well. Ask, "Will this person make more money? Will this person contribute to the consciousness of my business?" That's the way we choose who we hire.

One day Dain and I were in a restaurant eating lunch, and we could hear the guy at the next table trying to convince a woman to take a different percentage on her sales. He said, "We'll give you 15 percent of your annual sales if your sales are over a million, and 10 percent if they're $500,000. You can make a choice. Which one do you want—the 10 percent or the 15 percent? If you don't make the million dollars, we'll only give you the 10 percent even if your sales are more than $500,000." He was setting her up to fail. He didn't offer her 15 percent of everything over $500,000, only on everything over a million. If she came close, but failed to meet the target of a million dollars, she was screwed.

Dain went over to the guy and offered to coach the woman for free, as it was an area he was thinking about going into, and the guy got mad. He said, "I'm a sales manager for a Fortune 500 company!" He was angry that Dain interfered because he had figured out how to cheat the woman and make her work harder. This is what many businesses do. Rather than rewarding the person that adds to their business, they punish their employees for not reaching a goal they pretty much know they can't reach, so they only have to pay them the smaller percentage. Why wouldn't you reward the people who work for you rather than punish them?

The question is, "Do you want to generate your business—or do you want to destroy your business?" This sales manager was basically destroying his. His Fortune 500 company may become a Fortune 200 company in the future.

Here are some other questions you can use to generate money in your business. They will help you to create the energy that generates the future of your business.

What can I do to increase my sales?

What can I do to increase the business?

What can I be, do, have, create, or generate today that will generate and create more business?

What can the business be, do, have, create, and generate today that will generate more business now and in the future?

Create the Future

If you truly wish to generate money in your life, you need look at what you are going to generate today and in the future. You recognize that you may not have all the money you'd like to have, but you know that you're willing to have x amount of dollars right now and that you wish to generate something different in the future.

Generating is being the charge or the battery that keeps everything running. If the battery runs down on your iPod, it won't work. If the battery runs down on your phone, it suddenly cuts you off. It's as if you are the electrical system for your life. You are the generator; you are the one that keeps everything running. There is a sense of ongoing creation.

We see people who decide, "If I provide this service for this person, he or she will give me money." Good, he or she will give you money. But you also need to ask, "Will this also generate something in the future?" It doesn't occur to many people to ask a question like this. They are only doing things for today. They aren't focused on generating in the future. People believe the future will take care of itself. That's the difference between getting money and having money. If you're going to have money, you've got to be willing to generate it today as well as in the future. Ask, "If I do this today, what will it create for me today and in the future?"

Completion vs. Contribution. We often see people who say, "I have to get the money to pay my rent," so they go out and make enough money to pay their rent. Once they've done that, they stop using their generative energy. They think, "Ah, that's handled. I've got the rent money. Now I can stop." That's not how it works. You don't have anything handled in your life; you are handling your life. Your life hasn't ended when you get something done. This idea puts you on a start-and-stop loop. When you live your life as though it has completion points in it, you diminish the amount of energy you are using, and your money flows slow down until the next emergency comes along and then you start generating like mad.

There is no completion in the universe. Does a molecule or an atom complete? Never. Energy can't be destroyed; it simply alters and changes. You have never completed anything in your life. You have only created new possibilities. Every time you look at something from a new place, you are contributing to a new possibility in your life or a new jumping off point for creating something greater. What if every time you completed something, you saw it not as a completion, but as a contribution? In truth, that's what it is. Everything you complete is a contribution to the next thing you generate. It keeps on going; it keeps on generating. Many people have been taught to do tasks to "completion," as if completion actually existed. It's all right to accomplish things, but when you do so, continue generating. Ask, "What greater thing can I generate and create now?"

We are taught that we always have to get things done. "What are you going to get done today?" Done. Completed. I have got that off my list. I used to wake up every morning and make a to-do list that was three pages long. I would work very dynamically to complete my list, but I got very little accomplished because my focus was on completion rather than generation. Once I began to operate in a different way and asked, "Okay, what is possible today?" I was able to see what the day wanted me to do and be instead of what I thought I had to do and be.

Paradoxical as it sounds, when you have too many things going on and you are not completing them, it's because you are not generating enough. You don't have enough going on in your life. You will get those things completed when you add more to your life. The question, "What can I add to my life?" is about generation. It's "What else is possible?"

Generating money for today is, "I need to get money for the house payment. I have to have enough money to pay off my car over the next five years. I've got to have x amount. I've got to have this, I've got to have that." If you don't plan for what you're going to have tomorrow, you won't be generating today for tomorrow. You'll just be getting by today. That's not generating your life. It's focusing on getting the money you need today in order to make sure you don't lose what you've got. Are you generating all the time? Is your life on a constant flow and a constant increase—or is it on a start-and-stop loop? You want your life to be on a continuous increase.

A shift in that perspective changes the way you look at things. Ask, "What if I looked at right now and how my choices are going to affect my future, as it relates to money?" That's the start. The change in perspective opens up your awareness. It's as if you are walking down a road and you don't see anything to your left or your right, because you decided you have to look straight ahead. Then all of a sudden, you have a shift in awareness. You look around you and say, "Wow! There are things to my left and to my right that I never saw before." Your perspective broadens when you decide, "I'm not going to just live my life for today, I'm going to put things into place that will generate the future that I'd like to have and enjoy." You can come into more awareness and shift your perspective so you can see what's to the left and the right by taking the perspective of "not just now, but also the future" and asking questions to generate money now and in the future.

You've got to understand that the way you generate a future with massive amounts of money is through what you choose every day. You choose it for now and the future. You can't catch up to the future because the future's always the future. That's the reason you have to ask, "What can I be, do, have, create, or generate today and in the future?" That question, by the way, is the way you want to start your day.

Immediate Results. A lot of people think about money in terms of outflow and inflow. They believe that if they outflow some effort that they will immediately inflow some great result financially— but that's not how it works. This point of view becomes a problem, because when they don't see immediate results, they invalidate their ability to generate money.

The energy you put out today may generate a huge amount of money, but you may not see it for six months. In the time between now and then, you might be tempted to think, "That didn't create any result. I didn't generate anything today. That means there won't be anything tomorrow." When you make a decision like this that is exactly what will happen. You have decided it didn't work, which means even if it was going to work in six months, you won't get the result. You destroy the result before you get it. You stop the generation you put into motion with decisions like, "That didn't create any result." This is one of the big differences between people who are successful in business and those who aren't. Successful people don't jump to that conclusion. They keep asking, "Well, what did that create?" and "What else is possible?"

You don't know what the result of your choices will be. Did you know, ten years ago, that the choices you were making would create the life you currently have? This is the reason you have to ask, "What can I be do, have, create, or generate today that will make money today and in the future?" You've got to be willing to generate it today and in the future, at the same time. People tend to think, "Well, I was going to do this, and it didn't work." "It didn't work" means "that is the end." It stops an energetic flow and all the future possibilities. "It didn't work" is not necessarily true. What is true is that it hasn't yet occurred. We see people do this all the time. You've got to uncreate the evidentiary contrivances that result in a lack of patience and the unwillingness to wait for what you have generated to show up.

When I first started Access, were there people who were just waiting to do Access classes? No! But I started talking to people. I called every person I knew for six months, and asked them how they were doing and what was going on in their lives, and I never said a thing about Access unless they asked me a question. When they asked me a question, I would tell them what I was doing, and I would ask, "Do you know anybody who might be interested in this?" Most of them would say, "No, not off the top of my head . . . Come to think of it, why don't I get some people together and you can do a demonstration, and I'll help you that way." By talking to people, I created the future. I never stopped the energy. There's a lady I talked to about Access for twenty years, and she finally started coming to classes. Do you have that kind of patience? Or do you think, "If it doesn't happen yesterday, it ain't happening?"

Have you decided your inflow is not faster than your outflow? All the evidentiary contrivances and DJCCs you have to make that so, will you destroy and uncreate all of that, please? Right and Wrong, Good and Bad, POD, POC, All Nine, Shorts, Boys and Beyonds.

Make a Demand. Some people continuously set goals for themselves. They say, "My goal is to have a million dollars in the next two years." The problem with setting goals is that goals can become limitations. Say you decide you want to have a million dollars. Okay, that's it. You've got a million dollars. Will you exceed that amount? No. That's because goal means the line or place at which a race or trip is ended. It comes from the Middle English word for boundary or limit.

If you meet your goal and don't acknowledge it, you'll have to destroy what you have so you can start over again to achieve the same goal. A target, on the other hand, is something you can shoot at continuously. If you fail to achieve a bull's eye, you can still keep shooting. A goal is a decision; a target is a question. Okay, what can I shoot at? It's more of a choice. You can shoot at other targets. You can have multiple targets.

There are people such as Tony Robbins who teach that you have to determine your purposes and create plans in order to achieve goals. They say you have to have plans, purposes, and goals so you can create a life that looks like x, y, and z. They teach, "You do this so you can get that." Have you ever tried to do these things? How well have they worked for you? This approach might work for people who approach life from the perspective, "I will do this, this, this, and this to get my money so I can retire and die," but most people find this approach doesn't work very well. It has nothing to do with you being in your life and experiencing the joy of your life. The only thing that actually works is making a demand.

When you get to the place where you're willing to make a demand, things change. Have you ever been in a relationship that wasn't working for you? You weren't really happy with it, but you didn't want to change it, so it just went on the way it was. And finally one day you got fed up and said, "This has got to change. Either this changes or I'm killing myself. I don't care which it is." And all of a sudden it changed. That's the potency that happens when you make a demand.

We are talking about demanding what you desire of yourself—or of your business. We're not talking about making a demand of others. It's not about demanding that other people do it right, or get it right, or deliver what you need. The only person you can actually change is you. You've got to make a demand of you, "Okay, that's it. No matter what it takes, this is changing."

You don't judge yourself. You don't vilify yourself or make yourself wrong. You simply demand change of yourself. "No matter what it takes, I'm going to have my own source of money within the next year. I'm going to have the life I would truly like to have."

You have to get to the point where you say, "I'm not going to live like this anymore. I don't care what it looks like, it's going to be different." Don't try to fix something that's not working. If something in your life doesn't work, make a demand and do something different. The demand you make is what creates your future. "I demand, no matter what it takes, that I'm changing my current financial situation. It's going to be different." Don't say, "It's going to be better." Why not? Because better is a judgment. Better is based on the reference point of what you had, whereas different is based on no reference point. You've got to make a demand that no matter what, you're going to create a different future.

When you're not generating what you want in life, you'll come up with a thousand justifications for why you aren't doing it: "It's too hard." "It won't work." "I tried that once before." Are justifications the way to change things? No! You just have to make the demand, "I'm doing this no matter what." When I got to the point where I was going to do Access, I said, "I don't care what it takes, I'll do it."

To request something is pathetic. Demand it. "I'm having it—and that's it." Have you ever been in a restaurant and requested a glass of water, "Please sir, can I have some water?" and the waiter ignored you? You asked again, "Please sir, can I have some water?" and he ignored you. And then you said, "I'd like some water now, please!" Did he ignore you? No. That's a demand.

People ask, "Do I make the demand of myself or do I make the demand of the universe? The answer is: You demand, period. Me, myself, and I, and the universe too. Everything. "I demand that this change, now."

Making a demand is the first step. Then you have to ask, "What's it going to take for ____ to show up in my life?" or "What's it going to take to change this?" The question opens the door to seeing different possibilities. When you do this, things get better and opportunities will start to show up. Money will come to you from unexpected places.

Put the universe to work on your behalf. Are you worried by the financial turmoil that's going on in the world right now? Can't figure out what to do and how to overcome it? You don't have to be the effect of these economic hard times. You have to make a demand. You say, "You know what? Enough of being the effect of this financial stuff that's stressing everybody out and making people want to kill themselves. My life is going to change. I will change these points of view, in order to have my life be different for me." When you do this, you put the universe to work on your behalf, and you put your awareness to work on your behalf, so you can change things. You don't have to know how to change things right now. You just have to make the demand, "This is going to change," and then the how shows up. But until you make the demand, the how can never show up for you, because you're too busy buying the idea your money situation can't change.

What demand are you not making of you, that if you would make that demand of you, would manifest as too much money in your life? Everything that doesn't allow that to show up, will you destroy and uncreate all of that? Right and Wrong, Good and Bad, POD, POC, All Nine, Shorts, Boys and Beyonds.

What are you not demanding of your business, that if you demanded it, would manifest as too much ease and too many possibilities? Everything that doesn't allow that to show up, will you destroy and uncreate all of that? Right and Wrong, Good and Bad, POD, POC, All Nine, Shorts, Boys and Beyonds.

My life is going to be more like that. Because Dain and I use the tools we've described above, everything we ask for shows up in our lives. One of the things I've been asking for recently is a Dutch marquetry desk with an over-hutch. I've decided I'm going to replace a piece of furniture that's in my bedroom and put the desk in its place. The other piece of furniture is ready to leave my life. Why it's ready to leave, I have no idea, but it is. So I said to it, "You want to leave? You don't get to go until you find me a replacement. You've got to find me a Dutch marquetry desk at a really good price. Until then, you're stuck with me." One day I'm going to walk into a place and there's going to be a Dutch marquetry desk for a reasonable sum, and I'll say, "I'll take it."

Recently Dain and I were looking for a rug to cover the floor in our office space. We had a small rug in there, but it wasn't working, and we wanted a bigger rug to fill the whole space. We figured that we needed a rug that was nine by twelve. About three days later we were driving down the street and we saw a rug on the side of the road next to an old couch. They were free to whoever wanted to take them away.

I said, "That rug looks pretty nice." We picked it up, had it cleaned, and put it down in the office. It looked good. A few days later a painter walked into our office and said, "Wow, that's a Tibetan rug. I didn't know they made them that size." Cool! So now we have a giant Tibetan rug in our office that we got for free. We weren't interested in having a special Tibetan rug; we just wanted a rug that was the right color, the right size, and the right texture. We liked the fact that it was thick and plush. The purpose of things is to enhance your life. The things you would like to have will come into your life if you are willing to ask the universe to show you the opportunities. Are you willing to do that?

Even if you weren't willing to do that five seconds ago, what about right now? What if you read the story about the rug and said, "My life is going to be more like that. I'm going to have that. I'm going to have a life that I actually enjoy."

There is a process you can use to help develop this point of view. You need to use it thirty times a day for the next six months. What generative energy, space, and consciousness can I be that would allow me to be the energy of having and accumulating money I truly be? Everything that doesn't allow that to show up, will you destroy and uncreate it? Right and Wrong, Good and Bad, POD, POC, All Nine, Shorts, Boys and Beyonds.

Chapter 6

The Third Element of Generating Wealth

EDUCATE YOURSELF ABOUT MONEY AND FINANCE

If you wish to create the financial reality you desire, it is essential to educate yourself about money and finance. Most of us weren't taught anything about money except to work hard and save—and to be secretive about anything that has to do with money. No one teaches you how to deal with money. They give you no education about money in school. Your family gives you no education about money at home. You're fortunate if you are taught how to balance your checkbook. Some people don't even know how. They go on approximations. "I have approximately x amount of money in the bank." Then, when they bounce a check they ask, "How did that happen?"

There are three distinct and important parts of educating yourself about money. The first is to start stripping away all the false information—the piles of debris—you've taken in from others. The second is to find out how much money you have, how much you owe, how much you spend, and how much you need to generate each month. The third is to get the information you need to effectively function in your life with money.

AEIOU Pods, the Piles of Debris You Bought From Others

A   Asinine piles of debris you bought from others

E   Erroneous piles of debris you bought from others

I   Idiotic piles of debris you bought from others

O   Obnoxious piles of debris you bought from others, and

U   Useless piles of debris you bought from others

Did your parents tell you how to generate and create lots of money? Did their advice include statements like "work hard and save" or "buy the cheapest thing"? That is usually the sum total of education about money that kids get. It's not really education. It is fixing a point of view in kids' universes so they adopt the same viewpoints their parents have. The idea is to make them turn out the same as the parents.

When I was a kid, my mother used to tell me and everybody else who was listening that I would never have money because I was too generous: "Gary will never have money because he gives away all of his money. He just doesn't know how to hold on to money; he is way too generous." Did I come away thinking it was wrong to be generous? No, I came away convinced that I was going to prove her wrong. But that's the way I am. I am obnoxious and obstreperous; I like to go against what people say I am going do. Did your parents try to brainwash you into what they thought was correct economic information? A good one in my family was, "If we deprive you of what you desire, you will then learn the value of things." Before you buy your parents' AEIOU Pods, look at their lives. Have they lived the life you'd like to live? If they haven't, then you want to get rid of their points of view!

AEIOU Pods take many different forms. When you grow up in a lower-class neighborhood, for example, you know you're not allowed to have money. When you grow up in a middle-class neighborhood, you know that if you work hard and save a lot, you might get some money. And when you grow up in an upper-class neighborhood, you know that if you're not careful, you're going to lose it all. And no matter what kind of neighborhood you grow up in, you learn that money is something you don't talk about. It's secret!

We know a man who grew up in a wealthy, upper-class Jewish neighborhood. All the people around him were Jewish, but his family was middle-class Italian Catholic. He bought the point of view that only Jews get rich. He couldn't conceive of a Jew who wasn't rich. And since he wasn't Jewish, it was clear to him that he would never be wealthy.

I had a friend whose father invented things. The father loved inventing. He'd make a whole bunch of money on one of his inventions and then he'd give it all away. Then he'd invent something else. One year the family would be living in a mansion and the next year they'd be in a shack. The following year, they'd be in a mansion again, and the next, in a shack. This was the cycle of their life. My friend grew up with the idea that you either had feast or famine. Unfortunately, his dad dropped dead right after he gave away a $10 million business. Ah damn, so the family had no money. It was famine.

Another friend told us that when she was in graduate school, she bought into the Buddhist idea of non-attachment as well as the Marxist view that we should all be the same and that the consumer society is the root of all evil. She now wonders how her decisions about money have affected her financial situation.

There are also piles of debris that we take in energetically at a very young age. For example, many of us have parents who weren't doing well financially when they were young—which is just about the time we were born. If this is true of you, then from the age of zero to two, at a time when you weren't perceiving any difference between yourself and your parents, your parents were struggling financially. The thing is, when you're a kid, you're psychic. You pick up on the vibration of what's going on around you; if the people around you are struggling or having difficulties, then you perceive that life seems to be a struggle. Unfortunately many of us then lock this perception of life as a struggle into our own lives. We continue the financial struggle our parents had and maintain the limitations they had in place when we were very young children.

These are all AEIOU Pods.

What did your parents tell you about how to generate and create lots of money? Every AEIOU Pod you bought from your parents, will you destroy and uncreate it all? Right and Wrong, Good and Bad, POD, POC, All Nine, Shorts, Boys and Beyonds.

Every AEIOU Pod you bought from your parents, your religion, your neighborhood, or your social class, will you destroy and uncreate it all? Right and Wrong, Good and Bad, POD, POC, All Nine, Shorts, Boys and Beyonds.

Your Personal Finances

You are not going to become educated about money by reading the financial pages of the newspaper. Most economic theory is based on economists' ideas about consumption and debt, and what they're concerned about is how to maintain consumption—how to keep consumption going so the economy continues to run. You have to educate yourself about what having money is—not how to function within the supply and demand of economic theory, which is what the financial pages talk about. That's not educating yourself about money; that's learning how to get in line with the sheep at the trough where they get enough to eat.

We are suggesting you take a different approach to educating yourself. The first thing you need to do is find out how much money you have, how much you owe, how much you spend, and how much you need to generate each month.

How much money do you have? Balance your checkbook so you know how much money you have. Be aware of where you are financially at all times.

What is your net worth? What are your assets worth? You want to have assets, as assets are the foundation of your wealth. Until you own things that have some sort of intrinsic value in other people's worlds, you don't have a basis for your so-called net worth. Net worth is what you get when you add up your assets and subtract your liabilities. The asset column should be greater than the liability column. If it's not, then you're out of balance, and that's something you need to change.

Add up the value of everything you own. You need to be aware of how much money you actually have, and see if it's enough for you. Some people are happy with having basically nothing. It's okay with them to have a house and a car that they are making payments on. They feel secure because they have a roof over their head and nobody can kick them out or raise the rent. They don't ask whether those things are assets or liabilities. But this is something you need to look at.

Many people are afraid that if they look at their finances, they'll be so terrified that they won't be able to move, and everything will get much worse. That's functioning from anti-consciousness.

They're refusing to be aware of their money situation. But once you are aware of what it truly is, then you can change it. If you want to get to Tokyo, you need to know whether you're in Singapore or Montana. You need to know where you are, so you know in which direction to head.

Are you making payments on your house? What is your house worth if you were to sell it today? How much do you owe on it? If you were to sell it, would you make any money after you pay the realtors' commissions and all of the expenses associated with the sale? Are you making car payments? You might say, "Oh, I've got a great car" and that's fine—except you need to know that the value of it goes down every year. Does the amount you owe on it go down at the same rate as its value? More often than not, it's only the last two years of a five-year car loan that you start paying off the principal. Until then, you're paying the interest. You have to look at these things and see how they really are.

What is the value of the other things you own? I invest a lot of my money in antiques because I like them and they give me a lot of pleasure. If I'm having a bad money day, I go around my house and add up the value of everything I own, which I could sell for at least half of what I paid for it. After I look around long enough, I'll say, "Oh, it's fine!" I know that I have enough.

The joy of money is not so much about spending it but having everything around you have an intrinsic value. This is part of educating yourself about money. If you are interested in art, then surround yourself with really good art. Start educating yourself about what good art is, what its value is, and start collecting it. Surround yourself with things that have an esthetic vibration that matches yours.

How much money does it cost you to live each month? When we say you need to educate yourself, we are not talking about learning how to budget. It's not about having a budget or not. Living within a budget is a great idea, but what does that have to do with generating money? You want to have a budget only in the sense that you want to know how much money you have to generate. Budgeting doesn't help you create a life, but it helps you contextualize a life into what you have. You don't want to just fit into what you have. You want to create your life, grow your life, and move your life into greater heights. Do you see the difference? However, you do need to sit down and write out how much it costs you to live per month. That's your rent, utilities, gasoline, clothes, entertainment, and other monthly expenses. On top of that, add the 10 percent you are going to tithe to the Church of You.

If you have a partner, you either have to do this together, or you do yours separately and your partner does his or hers separately. If you do yours separately, you have to ask, "Does my partner come up with all the money he or she needs per month—or do I have to supplement his or her income?" If that's the case, then add in the amount of supplemental income you contribute in order to make things work.

One of my ex-wives spent every penny we had before we got it. I separated my finances out from hers, but she would call me periodically and ask, "Do you have an extra $900—or an extra $9,000? The bank bounced a check on me and I need to cover it." She never bounced a check her entire life; the bank bounced them.

I realized I had to have x amount of dollars in my account to cover the checks she would bounce every month. There was a point in our lives when we were spending between $1,200 and $3,000 a year in bounced-check charges. This is an example of a situation where you have to make a demand. When you get to the point where you say, "This is changing," it changes. At this point, you don't know how it's going to change; it doesn't matter how. You make the demand first— then the how shows up. "That's it, I'm changing this part of my life. I'm not going to throw this money away."

Figuring out what it costs you to live each month allows you to see where you're spending money. Let's say that you're spending $8,000 a month on clothes. You can ask yourself, "Do I really need $8,000 worth of clothing every month?" If the answer is no, ask yourself, "Is there a way that I could restructure this so I have fewer payments, less outflow, and more income?"

Someone asked me, "How do you live in abundance without spending money?" Being abundant is not about not spending money, it's about recognizing where you wish to spend your money and how you spend your money, and what you get out of it. This is the reason we ask you to figure how much money it takes to run your life every month.

My Money vs. His Money or Her Money. When we talk about spending money, people who are in relationships often ask us about "my money" vs. "his money" or "her money." Sometimes they feel tied to their partner and unable to make a money-related decision on their own. Whenever they spend money, they have to think about the other person and whether that person would be in agreement with their decision, and that makes them uncomfortable. We encourage people to have separate accounts in addition to their joint accounts so that they have the freedom to choose whatever they want; however, for some people, this is not easy. And yes, when you are in a relationship and sharing finances, you do have to consider the other person.

If you have a good, strong relationship, most of the time all you have to do is talk to your partner and say, "Hey, I found this thing I'd really like to have. Would it be okay with you if I spent x amount to get it?" Oftentimes the other person will say yes. It's just a matter of expressing what you would like to have and considering her or his feelings.

When I was married, my wife used to go out and spend $2,000 every weekend on clothes. She would buy clothes for me, clothes for our kids, and clothes for herself. She never asked if that was okay—she just did what she wanted with money, and that was part of what killed our relationship. She didn't include me in her choices about money.

I worried about what expenses I had to cover for my wife, what she needed, and what the kids were going to need. I knew what my employees were going to need, but I never brought myself into the computation. I never spent money on me. I felt it was somehow wrong. That unwillingness to spend money on you is called self-debting, and when you do that, you end up making you of no value. You don't want to make yourself of no value in the relationship. Don't make the mistake, even before you even talk to your partner, of deciding, "He or she wouldn't allow me to spend this amount of money, so I can't have it." It is not that you can't have it. It's that you have to be considerate of your partner's point of view. You just say, "Hey, I am thinking about this. Would it be okay with you?" Chances are your partner wants to give to you, too. Don't cut yourself out of the computation, but don't cut him or her out either. You want to make sure that this purchase is truly expanding your life and that you have sufficient assets to pay for it without creating a liability. All expenditures should expand your life in some way; they should not contract it.

Write down everything you spend money on. Many people throw money away; they do the strangest things with money. They don't actually use the money they have. Is this something you do? If you write down everything you spend money on for a week or a month, you may come to a new awareness of what you're doing with your money. Do you spend $3 on a cup of coffee, then let it get cold and throw it away after three sips? Do you buy a doughnut you don't even want? Is that where you want to spend your money? How often do you do this sort of thing? This kind of spending isn't even based on what you desire, and it doesn't provide you with any satisfaction or pleasure.

If you really want to educate yourself about money, get Jerrold Mundis' book, How to Get Out of Debt, Stay Out of Debt and Live Prosperously. He gives some tools you can use to get clear about what you're doing with your money. Is it a perfect book? No. But it will help you to become aware of what you're spending and how you're spending it, so that you understand where your money is going. You've got to get clear about where money is going. You can't say, "I want to have lots of money, but I don't want to change anything in my life."

How much money do you need to generate? Calculating your monthly expenses will give you an awareness of how much money you need to generate. Some people generate money for a particular item. They say, "I need this," and they generate money to handle that, but they forget about the rent. Then they say, "Oh, I forgot my rent," and generate money to get their rent. As soon as they have their rent, they forget to generate anything else.

Many people have no idea how much money they need to generate. You may have no idea what you would like to have in the way of money. When you have an overview of how much it costs you to cover all your monthly expenses, including your clothes and everything else, then you know what to ask for. Most people don't ask the universe for help in creating their money flows. You've got to be very clear about what you need. And then ask for help.

Money is the gasoline you need to get your engine going. If you don't have enough income, you're going to be short on how far you can go. If you don't ask for the number of gallons of money you need to get to where you want to go, guess what? You're going to run out before you get there.

You've got to be willing to ask in order to receive. Ask and ye shall receive. It's a quote from the Bible. Is it true or a lie? It's true. You've got to ask. If you don't ask, you don't receive.

What am I going to have to be, do, have, create, or generate in order to have this amount of money per month with ease? Let's say you're taking home $10,000 a month from your business, and you want more income. How do you approach that? You ask, "What can I be, do, have, create, or generate that would allow x amount of money to show up in my life?"

You may change the way you do business or you may change what your business does or you may change something in the business that starts to generate the money you require.

When you take the point of view, "I'm going to take this amount of money from my business," you have already created a limitation. What you want to look at is, "How much money can my business gift to me?" not "How much money can I take from it?"

How Do Things Function in This Financial Reality?

The third part of educating yourself about money and finance is learning how things function in this financial reality. You have to learn how banks, hospitals, insurance companies, taxes, credit cards, and all of those things work.

When you feel confused about your finances or anything else in your life, you aren't being functional. Feeling confused indicates that you need more information. Having enough information—and the correct information—helps you to be conscious in all areas of your life. It's what makes things work for you. And it's no different with money. When you don't understand an area, it's either because you don't have enough information, or you don't have the correct information. If I feel funky about something in my life, I call the lawyer, the doctor, the accountant, the Indian chief, or whoever can give me the information I need. This is how you become functional, because you can feel it when things aren't quite right. When you have the awareness that something isn't quite right or if you feel confused about something, ask, "What information do I need?" and "Who do I need to ask to get it?"

Credit Cards. It's important to learn how to effectively use your credit card. You should be able to pay off whatever you charge on your credit card each month. You should have enough money in your checking account to pay off your credit card balance in thirty days—or ninety days max. Otherwise, if you go out and charge a meal that costs you $40 and pay the minimum amount on your credit card, that meal will end up costing you $200 by the time you've paid interest.

The credit card system is currently set up so that if you're late two days on your payment, they can raise your interest rate as high as 32½ percent. Make sure you read your credit card bill every time you get it to see how much you've spent and what your interest rate is, because they may raise your rate. If you call them on it, they may lower it to 28 percent. The main thing is you want to get credit cards paid off as quickly as possible. Make it a policy to never charge items that cost more than you actually have. This is what people who have money do.

I use credit cards to pay business expenses. But if I want to buy toys, or if I want to buy antiques or jewelry, I pay cash for those. But really, it's not about using credit cards or not using credit cards. It's about being smart with credit cards and smart with cash.

Credit Card Debt. If you have credit card debt, you need to get it paid off. Look at the amount of money you owe on your credit cards, and ask, "How much more money would I have to generate each month in order to pay this sum off in one year?" It doesn't matter how much you owe. When you ask this question, you often find out it is not that much money. Look at how much you're earning on an hourly basis, and figure out how many more hours per month you would have to work to pay off your credit card balance in a year's time. If you are not making a sufficiently large hourly wage, ask, "What can I add to my life that would pay me a lot more money?"

If you have debt on more than one credit card, pay the smallest amount on the card with the lowest interest rate and the largest amount on the credit card that has the highest interest rate. Once you get the card with the highest interest rate paid off, cut it up and cancel it—or cut it up but keep the account open, as this may be better for your FICO score. Do what's going to work for you. Ask,

"Is it more appropriate to keep this account open? Is it going to be more rewarding to keep the account open? Is it going to make me more money to keep this account open? Or is it going to make me more money to close this account?"

If you have more than $15,000 or $20,000 in credit card debt, you might have to extend the payoff to two years. Figure out what it would take and how much you'd have to make to pay it off over two years. In the meantime, be aware that credit card companies can change the terms of your agreement at any time. Some of them are sending out notices of change of terms that state they are going to raise your interest rate unless you write to them and state that you are rejecting the rate increase. Many people don't read the notices they get from the credit card companies, so they have no idea their rates have been raised. And when they call, the company representative says, "Well, we sent you a notice, and you didn't do what you needed to do to keep your interest rate as low as it used to be, so you're out of luck." The companies can also change the minimum payment or raise the rate if you use your card for a new purchase, so carefully read the conditions in the pamphlets they send you.

Be aware that the government is not working on your behalf; it has eliminated usury laws, which means the credit card companies can now charge any amount of interest they choose. The credit card companies have become the new mafia. They got smart; they legalized their activities. And finally, if you need more specific help with paying off your credit card debt, get Jerrold Mundis' book, How to Get Out of Debt, Stay Out of Debt and Live Prosperously.

Taxes. Some people try to avoid paying taxes. Some even decrease their income dramatically so they will not have to pay taxes. This is not the best approach. You don't want to avoid taxes; instead, you want to use the tax system to your advantage. The system has been designed so people who have money can get out of paying taxes. Make it work for you. To do that, of course, you have to educate yourself about how it functions. Why continue to be a poor person who avoids paying taxes when you can become a rich person who doesn't pay any?

I worked with a lady who had a large income, but she had never educated herself about taxes. She didn't even know that mortgages were a tax write-off. She didn't know that if she paid somebody to work for her it was tax deductible—she could take the money out of Uncle Sam's pocket instead of her own. Every time she had to pay someone or write a check for her mortgage, she considered herself poverty stricken. She didn't realize how the tax system works in her favor, and the result was that she paid 38 percent of her income in taxes. Don't make mistakes like this. Find out how taxes work and use the system to your advantage.

Hospitals and insurance companies. You need to find out how hospitals, insurance companies, and other services function and whether they're going to be there for you when you need them. Do you think you can rely on insurance companies to take care of you in a time of crisis? Yeah, you can rely on the insurance companies. They're going to take great care of you. If you believe that, go talk to some of the victims of Hurricane Katrina. Do you know what they did after Hurricane Katrina? They offered people 10 to 25 cents on the dollar for what their houses were worth. Twenty-five cents on the dollar wouldn't rebuild most of them. Since the people turned that offer down, they had to go to court. They couldn't do a class action suit, so they have to be in court individually. The court system will be tied up for one hundred years handling all the cases from Katrina; meanwhile, the insurance companies have tripled their rates in all the areas that have hurricanes. They made a billion and a half dollars the year Katrina struck and they did not pay the $700 million in claims that were made against them. What are the insurance companies in business for? To make money.

And how do you even know the insurance company's going to be there when you're ready to collect? You don't. They can close on you. That is, quite literally, what they did after Katrina. If you live in California and you think you are covered in case there's a giant earthquake, you might want to reconsider. You've got to get realistic. Insurance companies are businesses; they are in business to make money. They don't want to pay you. They don't want to take care of you. They don't act on your behalf. They're there to screw you, so they can make money.

Right now I have a long-term health care policy for my ex-wife; it's one of the agreements I made in the divorce. It costs me $1,500 per quarter. That's $6,000 a year. She's sixty right now. If she doesn't begin to tap into this insurance until she's seventy, I will have paid $60,000 into it. That amount would keep someone in a facility for about one year. Most people in those facilities last one and a half to two years. This is the kind of information I need to make good choices. You've got to be willing to look at those things and decide what works for you. You've got to be prepared and aware.

Banks and the FDIC. Do you realize that when a federally insured bank shuts down, the government has seven years to return your money—and they don't have to pay interest? They will only pay you the amount you deposited. That's why they call it deposit insurance, not federal money insurance. And everything that's in a safe deposit goes to the bank.

If you choose to buy gold, purchase it and carry it around with you or keep it in your house. If it's in a safety deposit box when a bank closes, the government could pull the move they did in the 1930s and say, "You need to give all the gold back to the government, and we're going to give you x dollars for it." That is part of the 2001 Act; they can take all precious metals now, unless they are coins minted prior to 1933. If you buy gold or silver with numismatic value, they can't take them away—but you should keep any other precious metals in your possession.

All the AEIOU Pods you've bought about banks, insurance companies, the government, and how those good people are going to take care of you and make sure that you get treated right, will you destroy and uncreate all of that? Right and Wrong, Good and Bad, POD, POC, All Nine, Shorts, Boys and Beyonds.

Investing money. You also need to get clear about how investing works. Let's say you inherit some money. You can dig a hole and put it in the back yard or you can invest it. When my mother died and left me some money, my ex-wife decided that our money would grow if we put it into stocks. The guy we invested with was a shyster, and all the money disappeared. I didn't want to put the money into stocks in the first place. I wanted to put it in gold, but I let her talk me into investing it. Was I smart? No, I was stupid. I didn't listen to me; I went along with what she needed, valued, and desired. What I should have done was ask the money, "Where can I put you so you will grow for me?"

Hard currencies. You've also got to be willing to educate yourself about hard currencies. Hard currencies are things that can be turned into cash pretty much immediately. The reason I buy antiques is because they're a hard currency. I can sell any antique I have tomorrow for at least half of what I paid for it when I bought it. If I bought it ten years ago, I'll double or triple my money.

Buy things that have intrinsic value. Dain grew up in a home where all the furniture was in matching sets from Levitz. He says that the first time he walked into my house, which was full of antiques, he looked around and thought, "This house is full of old stuff that doesn't match." His viewpoint was that if it wasn't from IKEA or Levitz, it had no value. As he started educating himself about what had value, he realized that my "old stuff" was not only beautiful; it was also worth a lot of money. He saw that my antiques were assets. They had intrinsic value. They could be sold for a good amount of money unlike the things in his family's home, where the most expensive thing in the house was the stove or the refrigerator.

You want the things you buy to have value. This is another aspect of having money. These are all examples of why you have to be willing to educate yourself about how these financial things work, so that you know what's going on.

Chapter 7

The Fourth Element of Generating Wealth

GENEROSITY OF SPIRIT

The fourth element of having money is generosity of spirit. Generosity of spirit is a way of being in your life. It's about living your life with a sense of joyful generation. One of the big things you can do to increase your generosity of spirit is learn to gift.

Gifting

Most so-called giving usually involves a desire to get something in return, but a true gift carries no sense of obligation. We suggest that you learn to gift without any expectation of getting something in return. You don't have to have millions stored away in your bank account before you buy someone lunch or give them a gift that will make them happy or change their reality. The paradox of this kind of gifting, where there is no expectation of a return, is that you receive energetically. Your life expands when you adopt the point of view of generating something different in another person's reality.

At Christmas time, Dain and I give $500 to a lady in Mexico whose husband was killed in a truck hijacking on Christmas Eve. She has two little boys, and she makes about $50 per month, or $600 per year. We started giving her money every year for Christmas, and the condition is that she spends half of it on Christmas for the boys. She can do whatever she wants with the other half, but the first half has to be spent on the boys. She calls us los angeles. We are the angels in their lives who make sure that they have Christmas. She has never met us. We know her brother, but we've never met her or the boys. Doing things like this changes people's reality about money. Five hundred dollars to change somebody's reality. Is it worth it? Yes! Gifting in this way changes our lives so much. We receive dynamically when we do this, and our lives expand. Her gratitude is a contribution to our sense of well being, and we appreciate our ability to do this. It's not about huge amounts of money; it's about our ability to do it. You can do this kind of gifting in large and small ways.

Dain and I recently flew in to Los Angeles from Costa Rica, and we were on the bus to get our rental car. We had five heavy suitcases loaded onto the bus, and when we got out, the driver helped us put them into the car. I was going to give him a $5 tip, a dollar for each bag, but instead I gave him a $10 bill. You would have thought I'd given him the Taj Mahal. He was stunned. It changed his whole day that someone would give him $10 as a tip. Here was a sweet guy who was doing his best in a job that doesn't pay him all that much, and he wanted to be caring and giving to us. Why the heck wouldn't you give back?

While we were waiting in the airport, we saw a lady who was doing shoe shines. I said, "Let's get our shoes shined." While the lady was shining Dain's shoes, he asked her, "So, how long have you been doing this?"

She said, "Oh, about three years."

He asked, "Do you like it?"

She said, "Yeah, because I can do it during the day and go to nursing school at night."

Dain said, "Oh, cool!"

The shoeshine was $4. Dain flipped through his wallet and he handed her $100. He said, "That's for you."

She looked at him and couldn't even talk. It blew her whole universe apart. She said, "Thank you so much! I don't know what to say! This has never happened to me! This is amazing. Everything is going to be okay!"

Then he gave her a hug and said, "You know what? You are going to make such a difference in the world. You're going to be a great nurse. Keep going!"

It was a genuine receiving and blowing apart of her universe.

The bottom line is that there is really only one reason to have money, and that's to change other people's realities. When you have money, you can change other people's realities in a heartbeat. What happens when you give something to someone that they didn't expect or didn't feel they deserved? You change their reality. And what is the value of changing other people's realities? You show them there is a different possibility, and in this way, you advance consciousness and mankind.

Once in New York City, I was on my way to lunch, and I walked past a guy who was begging for money. He had a big, open gash in his leg. He asked, "Please, can you help me out here?" I took $50 out of my wallet and put it in his can as I walked by. He looked at it and he said, "Bless you sir, bless you!" He never looked up and saw me. He never saw my face; he never saw any part of me. All he saw was the $50 in his can. The change in his energy was huge. Interestingly enough, I never saw him in that place again. Could $50 change somebody's reality? You never know what it's going to take to change somebody's reality. It's not the amount you give; it's that you give without expectation, without need of return, without anything other than the idea that you're doing something to change another person's reality.

You're not doing it because you feel superior or because you think you're being generous or because you think you have more money than they do. You're doing it because it makes you feel good and because you are interested in changing someone's reality.

Several years ago, I bought a horse. If I had been thirty-five, he would have been the perfect horse for me. He would have been everything I ever wanted in a horse. At sixty, he was not the perfect horse for me, but I was still riding him. Dain and I would go out to ride our horses, and I'd run my horse, whose name is Playboy, around the ring before I rode him. Each time he came to Dain, he'd stop. He'd run around the ring once and stop in front of Dain and then run around the ring again and stop in front of Dain. I'd beat him off of Dain every time he did this.

Neither one of us asked a question like, "Why is he doing that?" We just thought, "That's weird."

One day Dain and I were going out for a ride in the backcountry, and Dain said, "Please can I ride Playboy? I want to ride him. Please can I ride him?"

Playboy is an ex-race horse. If you put him into a gallop, he goes to a dead run—and from a dead run, he covers the ground at the speed of light. Only someone who knows how to ride very well should ride him.

At the time, Dain was not much of a horseback rider, and I thought, "Let's see. What's the worst thing that can happen? He could fall off and break some bones. I can take my cell phone with me, so I can call in a helicopter in case he gets badly hurt, but I can fix pretty much anything else with the body processes we have in Access," so I said, "Okay, fine."

Dain got on Playboy, and Playboy turned around and looked at him and said, "My man."

I said, "Say what? You're my horse!"

And Dain looked at Playboy and said, "I love him so much!" He was in tears. He had just gotten on the horse! He hadn't yet ridden him any place. Dain was sitting on the horse and the reins were hanging down to the ground, and he kicked Playboy into a canter. He had no hold on Playboy's mouth. He had no control. It was as if he was expecting Playboy to be a merry-go-round horse. I thought, "Dain's dead." What happened? Instead of breaking into a dead run—whonk-whonk-whonk, Playboy started cantering slowly—gloppity-gloppity-glop.

I suddenly realized, "This is Dain's horse. These two need to be together." So I made Dain a deal he couldn't refuse. I gave Playboy to him. At the time, Dain didn't have much money. I said to him, "I have a gift for you. I'm giving you Playboy."

Dain says his universe exploded at that point. This horse was willing to be sold for $15,000. In effect, Dain had just received a $15,000 gift. It totally changed his reality. He says that the reverberations of it are still in his universe. It opened him up to a level of receiving that he didn't even know could even exist. My world keeps expanding because I'm willing to expand other people's realities. Whatever I do with money, it's to expand others' realities, not to make mine better. That's generosity of spirit.

Being Grateful When Others Receive

Generosity of spirit is not only about what you give; it's also the willingness to have others receive in every aspect of their life. It is about being happy and grateful when others receive, whether you do or not. A lady recently called me and said, "I'm going to tell you this because no one else in the world would be happy for me.

Twenty years ago, my roommate wrote up a will leaving his money to me and his other roommates. He never changed his will, and he just died in an accident. I just got $10,000 as a result of the will that he made twenty years ago."

I said, "That's great! I'm so happy for you." I'm happy when other people get something. I'm not envious of them. I don't think they got something I deserved. Generosity of spirit is being grateful and thrilled she received that money.

How about you? Do you feel a sense of gratitude and happiness when others receive things? Or do you create the evidentiary contrivances and DJCCs that say if they get something, it means you didn't get it? Everything that is, will you destroy and uncreate it all? Right and Wrong, Good and Bad, POD, POC, All Nine, shorts, Boys and Beyonds.

If you realize that you get a contracted feeling when others have good fortune, you can recognize it and say, "I've created selfishness. My point of view is that if they get it, I don't." The cool thing is that you can recognize it with no judgment. This is your chance to change it. Any point of view you have can be changed. What would it be like if, instead of judging you, you could say, "Yes, I've been selfish," or "I've considered myself selfish a lot of my life. I'd like to change that now" or "I was being selfish. Is that limiting me in my life? Is it limiting the money I can have? Yes! What would it be like to have a greater point of view that would actually generate more that I'd like to have in my life?"

People who truly have money do not need to put other people down. They do not need to live as if they were superior to anyone. Many people who are wealthy complain about their servants. They are never grateful for anything anybody does. They "know" they deserve to have more and that everybody is cheating them by not delivering a good enough product. When you're truly willing to have money, you're grateful for everybody who gifts anything to you. I'm grateful for the waiter who does a good job. I'm grateful for the maid who does a good job. I'm grateful for the people who take care of our horses and do a good job, and because of my gratitude, they're grateful to work for me. They try to see what else they can do for me.

When you have money, you're grateful for the people who show up in your life and you're grateful for what they do for you. But when you have to get money, you assume you're being cheated somehow. Getting money is more important to you than having money. Do you see the difference here? It is an important distinction. You don't have to have money in order to have gratitude. But if you have gratitude, the generosity of spirit that comes with gratitude starts to generate more money in your life.

Being Generous with Yourself

Generosity of spirit also includes the willingness to receive. Are you generous with yourself in your life? Generosity is a willingness to be kind to yourself as well as everybody else. We want you to add a new verse to your personal Bible: "'Tis as blessed to give, as it is to receive." Both giving and receiving are blessed events.

Be grateful for what other people get, but also be grateful for what you yourself generate—because you are much more amazing than you give yourself credit for. Living in a state of gratitude is one of the greatest ways of having a life you enjoy as well as increasing your ability to receive and be. Living in a state of gratitude puts you in the flow of the universe, where generation is possible. It takes you beyond contextual reality, beyond "How am I going to win? How am I going to lose?" Gratitude catapults you beyond all that into non-contextual reality and awareness, which is where the questions, the possibilities, the choices, and the contribution lie.

Here are three questions you can use to help you develop greater generosity of spirit.

1. What would it take for me to be the generosity with money I truly be and haven't acknowledged? Everything that is, will you destroy and uncreate it all? Right and Wrong, Good and Bad, POD, POC, All Nine, Shorts, Boys and Beyonds.

2. What generative energy, space, and consciousness can I be that would allow me to be the generosity of spirit with money that I truly be and don't ever acknowledge? Everything that is, will you destroy and uncreate it all? Right and Wrong, Good and Bad, POD, POC, All Nine, Shorts, Boys and Beyonds.

3. Everything that keeps you from the gratitude for you that would change your whole financial life, and all the thoughts, feelings, emotions, and no-sex you're using to destroy, compress, or kill the gratitude you could have for you, will you destroy and uncreate it, please? Right and Wrong, Good and Bad, POD, POC, All Nine, Shorts, Boys and Beyonds.

Additional Tools
You Can Use
to Generate Money

Additional Tools
You Can Use
to Generate Money

If Money Weren't the Issue,
What Would I Choose?

One day I went with Dain when he was looking for a new fax machine. He was looking at all the different machines, and I asked him, "If money weren't the issue, what would you choose?"

His first thought was, "If money weren't the issue, I'd choose the most expensive machine." He was standing in front of an all-in-one machine that was about $550. He looked at it and said, "That's the one. If money weren't the issue, that's the one I would choose."

Then he saw another fax machine around the corner. It was $150. As he looked at it, he realized the $550 machine was too big to fit under his desk; it actually wouldn't fit anywhere in his office. The smaller one was the perfect size. It would fit under his desk, right where he wanted it, and it had all the functions he needed.

He said, "Wow, I just saved $400 by asking this question."

Most of us make our buying decisions based on money. We say, "I can't afford this, therefore I'll put it on a credit card" or we say, "I can't afford this, so I won't buy it." We don't ask, "Do I truly wish to have this?" or "Is this really necessary for my life?"

Depriving yourself of something that will expand your life is not the way to make things better in your life, but this doesn't mean you should overextend and overspend either. It's not about always choosing the best; it's about recognizing, given the current circumstances, what the best choice is for you. If the best I can afford is Veuve Clicquot Champagne, I will choose that. I will wait for Dom Pérignon to happen later, when I have more.

When you ask, "If money weren't the issue, what would I choose?" you take money out of the computation as the determining factor for choice. This question provides a different way of looking at the world and understanding what you'd truly like to have in your life.

Most people's sense of valuing something is based on their inability to have it or pay for it. You look at something and it seems valuable to you because you believe you can't afford it—but you buy it anyway. What happens when you do this? A week later you totally forget about it. You've spent a lot of money and now you're paying it off on your credit card.

Here's something you can do: Go into the most expensive store in town, look around, and acknowledge that you could have anything in the store if you truly chose to have it, even if you put it on perpetual layaway. Then look around and see what you truly desire to have. Even though you initially might have thought you wanted everything in the store, once you look around to see what you would truly like to have, you will probably end up deciding on the one thing you'd really like—or maybe nothing at all. More often than not, you'll discover that you really don't desire anything in the store. You only thought you desired it because you decided you couldn't afford it and it was going to fulfill some need for you.

The idea that buying something is going to fulfill some need is called retail therapy. How many evidentiary contrivances and DJCCs do you have that say retail therapy makes you feel good? Everything that is, will you destroy and uncreate it all? Right and Wrong, Good and Bad, POD, POC, All Nine, Shorts, Boys and Beyonds.

Or you may have evidentiary contrivances about what you can't have, based on other people's points of view. Maybe you had a mother who questioned you every time you bought something with some version of the question, "Do you really need that?"

How many evidentiary contrivances do you have that are based on other peoples' points of view that invalidate the choices you made? Everything that is, will you destroy and uncreate it all? Right and Wrong, Good and Bad, POD, POC, All Nine, Shorts, Boys and Beyonds.

How Does It Get Any Better Than This?

Every time you find a penny, a dime, a dollar, ten dollars, or any other sum large or small, ask, "How does it get any better than this?" Acknowledge what you have, and the fact that it can get better. If you say, "Oh good! Look what I've got!" or even "Wow, thanks universe, I got it!" the universe says, "Oh, you got it. I don't have to contribute to you anymore." But when you ask, "How does it get any better than this?" it keeps the energy moving.

Our friend Simone has a friend in Australia who is a musician. She told him about using "How does it get any better than this?" and he decided to try it after a concert when he was selling his CDs. He sent a text to her the next day and said, "This stuff really works! Every time I sold a CD, I asked, 'How does it get any better than this?' and somebody else would come up and buy one or two. I ended up selling all my CDs at the concert."

Use this when you pay bills, too. It's not, "Oh no! There's not enough money to pay this bill." Every time you pay a bill, ask, "How does it get any better than this?" We often see people who get almost enough money to pay a bill, and they say, "Whoa, this isn't enough!" What does this do? It puts a stop to the energy they were generating. What would happen if instead they asked, "How does it get any better than this?" They would create an invitation for more of that energy to come into their lives.

A young lady we know told us she was recently checking her bag at the airport, and the guy at the counter said, "Your bag is twenty pounds overweight. I'm going to have to charge you for this."

She smiled and asked, "How does it get any better than this?" and "What else is possible?"

The guy said, "Just a minute, please," and he came back with his supervisor. The supervisor looked at her said, "Your bag is twenty pounds over. We're going to have to charge you for this."

She asked, "Okay, how does it get any better than this?"

The supervisor looked at her, said, "Oh, never mind," and sent the bag through without charging her.

Keep asking the question, "How does it get any better than this?" When you use it in what seems like a bad situation, you get clarity on how to change things, and when you use it in a good situation, all kinds of interesting things show up. The universe hears what you ask and provides what you ask for. But you've got to ask.

Interesting Point of View

When you are in a place of no judgment, you recognize that you are everything and you judge nothing, including yourself. There is simply no judgment in your universe. There is total allowance of all things.

When you are in allowance, you are a rock in the stream. Thoughts, ideas, beliefs, attitudes, and emotions come at you, and they go around you, and you are still the rock in the stream. Acceptance is different from allowance. If you are in acceptance, when thoughts, ideas, beliefs, and attitudes come at you, you get washed away. In acceptance, you either align and agree, which is the positive polarity, or you resist and react, which is the negative polarity. Either way, you get washed away.

If you are in allowance of what I'm saying, you can say, "Well, that's an interesting point of view. I wonder if there's any truth in that." You go into a question instead of a reaction. When you go into resistance and reaction, or alignment and agreement with points of view, you create limitation. The unlimited approach is "interesting point of view."

Every time you notice that you have a point of view about something, say "Interesting point of view that I have this point of view." You may think something is true or real, but it's only a point of view. It's not real. You make it real and right. You judge it into existence.

Let's say I'm not making the amount of money I'd like in my business. If I have the point of view, "My business is failing," I have created an evidentiary contrivance. I bring that reality into existence and begin to act as if it's real. Is my business failing? No. Is it making as much money as I'd like it to make? No. Will it ever make as much money as I'd like it to make? No. Okay, fine. Why not? Because no matter how much I make, I'll always desire more. If you find yourself with the point of view like "my business is failing," just recognize it and say, "Interesting point of view that I have this point of view." That's all you need to do.

"Interesting point of view" followed by a question is a great way to change a situation you'd like to be different. Say, for example, you have a big customer call and cancel her order. If you take the point of view that this is going to destroy your business, that's what you'll create. But if you say, "Wow, that's interesting she would do that!" and ask questions like "What other opportunities are available that we haven't looked at?" or "What could we do or be differently that would change this?" you open the door to a different reality.

I used "interesting point of view" with every point of view I had for a year until I had no point of view about anything. Now when I look at something, I have no point of view about it. This is great, because I can ask questions, and my point of view doesn't get in the way of hearing the answers. When I ask something, "Will you make me money?" I can clearly hear it when it says yes or no.

What Will It Take for _____ to Show Up?

"Ask and you shall receive" is one of the truths in the Bible. There's a lot of stuff in there that isn't true, but this is one of the truths—and it's one we tend to ignore. We don't ask for what we desire in life.

Sometimes when we are working with people on the subject of money, they'll ask, "Why can't I get out of debt? Why won't money show up so I can be happy?"

We'll inquire, "Well, have you asked for it?"

They will look at us, dumbfounded.

We will repeat the question, "Well, have you asked for the money?"

They'll say, "What do you mean?"

We'll answer, "You have to ask for something in order for the universe to work on your behalf, so you can have it."

And they'll say, "I have been working, I have been doing affirmations, I've been doing this, I've been doing that, and none of it is working."

And we'll say, "I know. It's because you haven't asked for the money."

We can't tell you how many people are doing everything right, but missing this one essential point. Once they understand this and start to ask the universe for what they desire, their financial situation starts to change.

A good way to ask for something is to say, "What will it take for _____ to show up?" For example, "What would it take for me to double my income this year?"

Instead of asking questions, most people make presuppositions. "The only way I can double my income this year is if I have two full-time jobs." The thing is, once you go into the presupposition mode and try to figure things out, then nothing else can show up for you. You've created a giant limitation. The way to generate what you wish to have is to simply ask the universe for what you desire. "What's it going to take for _____ to show up?" is an effective way of doing this.

Once you ask, however, you've got to be willing to do what it's going to take to generate the money you're looking for.

What Else Is Possible?

When you're in a situation that's not going the way you would like, try asking, "What else is possible?" For example, if I don't have as much money in the bank as I would like to have, the question, "What else is possible?" might open the door to a new possibility.

Use other questions like, "What else can I get? What can I change? What can I generate? What can I be? What energy can I be? What can I do?"

I don't have the point of view that anything will ever stop me, which is a demand, and I know I can use questions to discover a fresh viewpoint or to see an opportunity that wasn't visible previously.

How Did I Create This?

I was recently in Texas, driving with my friend Curry in a new car that she had bought for her son. I passed a coffee shop and I heard, "Let's get a cup of coffee." I thought, "I don't want coffee," and I kept on driving.

Then I heard, "Why don't you stop here at that antique shop?" and I didn't do it. Of course, it wasn't open.

A few minutes later, we came to a stoplight, and we were sitting next to a giant Texas truck that was eight feet off the ground. When the light turned green, the car in the lane next to me didn't move, so I pushed on the gas just a little bit and we started to creep forward. All of a sudden, boom! Somebody hit the front of our car and drove off as fast as they could go. Hit and run. They took off like a bat out of hell. Our car was badly crunched.

Now, if I had I listened and stopped at the antique shop, we wouldn't have been there when the car came barreling through the red light. Had I listened and stopped for a cup of coffee, we wouldn't have been there. But no, I didn't listen. I went against the information I was getting. I heard all the information that would have prevented this from happening, and I ignored it. Why did I ignore these subtle hints that I should have been listening to? When something like this happens, you have to ask, "I didn't listen for what reason?"

People pay dearly when they don't listen to the subtle hints they get. Sometimes the hints don't make sense, but you should listen anyway. It didn't make sense for me to get a cup of coffee. It didn't make sense for me to stop at the antique shop that was closed, but it isn't about sense: It's about awareness. Instead of continuing forward at the light, if I had asked, "What am I not being aware of here?" I would have taken the time to see that something didn't feel right. Even so, I didn't bolt into the intersection when traffic wasn't moving. Normally I tend to be a lead foot. I like to be hot off the mark. In this situation, I could have gotten out in front of the car ahead of us. Normally I drive that way, but for some reason I didn't do that on this occasion.

Curry said, "You were driving like an old man, and I didn't know what you were doing." I was driving like an old man so we wouldn't get killed. If I had taken off as soon as the light had changed, it would have been the other car's hood in my door. There are times when driving like an old man is a rightness.

After it happened, I looked back to see what occurred and to see why I hadn't paid attention to the subtle hints. I asked, "How did I create this?" I was looking for the ten seconds of unconsciousness that created that result.

The crash awakened me to the fact that I have to get even more intensely aware than I was before. As you become more aware, things come to you as a feather stroke rather than a two-by-four over the head. You've got to be willing to receive the feather strokes to know what's really going on, otherwise the two-by-four to the head is required. Asking the question allowed me to see how I chose to be unconscious about my awareness that we should take a break and get off the road. I created the situation by not paying attention to that awareness before the accident; if I had, it would have changed all that was going to occur.

All of the evidentiary contrivances and DJCCs you have to make all of your awarenesses come as a two-by-four, or an eight-by-eight, or an anvil between your ears, will you destroy and uncreate all of that? Right and Wrong, Good and Bad, POD, POC, All Nine, Shorts, Boys and Beyonds.

What's Right About This That I'm Not Getting?

After the car crash, Curry used this question to see what she hadn't been paying attention to. She realized her son didn't like the car. The crash awakened her to the fact that the car needed to be loved, and not just sit in the driveway. She said, "My son actually wanted a different car, but instead of getting him the car that he wanted, I bought him a car that worked for me."

"What's right about this that I'm not getting?" is a beautiful question to use with your money situation or any circumstance you're not happy with. It opens you to new ways of seeing what's going on in your financial world. Let's say you're about to lose your job, you don't have any prospects for a new one, and you aren't making enough money to cover your expenses. Things look bleak. You don't know how you're going to pay your bills next month. You don't seem to have any options. What's the first thing to do? Take a deep breath and then another and another. The first step is to come out of hyperventilating and into the present so you are willing to receive the information that comes up when you ask a question. Then ask, "Okay, what's right about this I'm not getting?" Did you want that job in the first place? Do you still want that job? If you take away the point of view that you are losing something valuable, what else might be possible?

Sometimes when we ask people, "Did you realize you are really done with that job?" they say, "I've been dying on the vine in that job!"

We say, "Cool, so what would you actually like to do?"

They say, "I don't know, but it would feel totally different."

We say, "Okay, then, go with that energy."

Ten-Second Increments

When you were a kid, and your parents took you to the ice cream store, did they say, "You can have anything you want" or did they say, "You can have this—or that"? Most parents ask, "Do you want this— or do you want that?" They give you two choices. But we didn't see why we had to choose between "this" and "that." We wanted it all!

Most of us have never been taught to choose for ourselves. As a result, we often have difficulty making choices when we become adults. In Santa Barbara, there's a restaurant that has a huge Sunday morning buffet. There is a mile-long table full of every kind of food you could think of. There's so much food, it would be impossible to have just one bite of everything. How do you possibly choose what to have? I walk in, I look at the table, and I'm done. I spend $55 just to look at all that food. We're told we have infinite choices, but we can't have any of them. We think it's easier to choose between two things. Will I have a scrambled egg or a piece of bacon?

Often we get into the situation where we are trying to make a choice between two things we don't even want. We try to figure out what is the lesser of two evils. It's like voting for a politician. There's no one you really want to elect, so you choose the one who is the least bad. This is what you've been taught to do. You don't choose that which will expand your life and give you everything you desire. You choose between what is awful and not quite that bad.

Instead of choosing between "this—or that" or struggling to make a choice when there are too many things to choose from or choosing the lesser of two evils, begin to do everything in ten-second increments. Instead of looking at all the men in the world and trying to find which one to love, or instead of trying to choose between two guys that you don't really want, just choose to love somebody for ten seconds. You can un-choose him ten seconds later. Or you can choose to love him again in the next ten seconds.

When you think a choice is the only one you will ever have, you tie yourself up trying to make the right choice. Instead, try ten-second increments of choice. The beauty of choosing in ten-second increments is that choice creates awareness. Most of us have been told to think about the consequences of our choices. People say, "Be careful what you choose because if you make a mistake, you can't turn back." Is that a truth? Does that make you feel light? Or does that make you feel heavy? Or does it send you into a panic? It makes you feel heavy, because it's a lie! You never know what's going to happen until you choose.

If you make a choice and don't like the consequences, say, "Oops, that was a bad choice. Next!" Choose again. When you operate in this way, there's no panic about choice, because the choice has no significance or meaning.

> Let's play a little game. You have ten seconds to live the rest of your life. You're in the jungle, and it's full of lions, tigers, bears, and poisonous snakes. It just looks like the city you live in. You're going to die here in the next ten seconds. You have ten seconds to live the rest of your life. What do you choose?

Maybe it goes something like this, as it did in a recent class:

> Gary: You have ten seconds to live the rest of your life. What do you choose?
>
> Participant: To make love.
>
> Gary: To make love. Okay, that should take a little longer than ten seconds. If it isn't, get a new guy.
>
> Participant: To eat something sweet.
>
> Gary: Okay, good.
>
> Participant: Freedom, liberation.
>
> Gary: Okay that lifetime is over. You have ten seconds to live the rest of your life. What do you choose?
>
> Participant: Joy. Fun. Money. Awareness.
>
> Gary: Good. That lifetime is over. Choose again!
>
> Participant: A bicycle.
>
> Gary: Good. That lifetime is over. Choose again!
>
> Participant: To play, to have a glass of wine.
>
> Gary: Good. That lifetime is over. Choose again!
>
> Participant: To take a beautiful photograph.
>
> Gary: Okay, that lifetime is over. Choose again. Did you notice that as you chose in ten-second increments you started to get lighter?

Do this all the time, every day. In one ten-second increment, you can say, "I hate working in this pharmacy." In the next ten seconds, you can say, "I love being a pharmacist! I love doing my job!" In one ten-second increment, you can say, "I hate this person I have to teach yoga to," and in the next, "I love the smell of this person I have to teach yoga to."

When you choose in ten-second increments, nothing sticks you. You take the point of view, "I want today to be a different day than yesterday." If I have a day where four people are scheduled for private sessions, and the first one calls and cancels, I say, "Okay universe, are you trying to tell me this is a day off?" If the answer is yes, I call the other three people, and 99 percent of the time they say, "Oh, I am so glad you called because I really didn't want to have a session today, but I had the appointment and you're so hard to get a hold of, I didn't want to cancel." They didn't want to do a session either. The universe was trying to tell me it was time to take a day off. I was willing to make a different choice—and so were they.

You can do this even when you have a so-called big or important decision to make, like your business is in the red and you don't have enough money and you need to decide what to do. Don't try to force something into existence so you can make a buck. Instead, choose in ten-second increments.

People have said to me, "Functioning in this reality requires a lot of planning. You can't always do things in ten seconds. If I buy an airline ticket ten seconds before the flight, I'm going to pay a lot more for it."

I say, "You can still make plans. I make plans to do all kinds of things, but I am also willing to change my plan in the next ten seconds. Just because I've made a plan doesn't mean I can't change it." Many people think they have to follow through if they make a plan. Have you been told that if you don't follow through you're a flake? If someone tells you you're a butterfly or a flake or a complete idiot, recognize that they're telling you about themselves. You can function in this reality and make plans in ten-second increments if you are willing to change. This makes your life easier. And if somebody tells you you're flaky or a butterfly, say thank you. They won't know what to do with that. It's always good to leave them with their mouths hanging open.

This reality is just what it is. You don't have to live in it, but you want to be able to function in it. When you function in this reality, you're functional. That means you are willing to look at what is, to know what you can change and what you cannot change, and to deal with everything as it is. When you are functional in this reality, you are aware you have other choices available. You look at things and say, "Everybody expects things to turn out this way. Do I have to live with what other people expect? Do I have to do things the way other people do them? Do I have to suffer the way other people suffer? No! I can have a different reality." Living in ten-second increments can help you to do this.

All of Life Comes to Me with Ease and Joy and Glory

And finally, in Access we have a mantra: All of life comes to me with ease and joy and glory. Ease is effortlessness; joy is happiness, pleasure, and delight; and glory is the exuberant expression and abundance of life that is possible.

Dain says that when he first heard "All of life comes to me with ease and joy and glory," he started saying it thirty times in the morning, thirty times in the evening, and at other times throughout the day, and it changed the energy he was willing to have in his life. He says, "Saying 'All of life comes to me with ease and joy and glory,' changed the space that I functioned from. When I first started to say it, I'd feel like there was no space in my life, but after saying it five or ten times, it opened up space."

It's amazing what kinds of things can happen when you say, "All of life comes to me with ease and joy and glory."

My oldest son used to be a drug addict. He went out with my car one night to supposedly get a pack of cigarettes, and he didn't come home. He was gone all night long. I didn't know what to do, so I just kept saying, "All of life comes to me with ease and joy and glory." I didn't feel that life was coming to me with ease and joy and glory; I just said it. I woke up at two o'clock in the morning and heard a car, and he wasn't home, so I said it again. I did it at four o'clock and again at six o'clock. Finally about 7:30 in the morning, he walked in the door. I said, "All of life comes to me with ease and joy and glory. Okay, what's the deal?" I had already told him that he had been doing drugs so long and was so out of control that he would have to leave our home the next time he chose that.

He said, "You know what? I need a drug program."

He had already been in three drug programs, but he had never chosen to go on his own. We had to force him into it. So, he went into a drug program for eighteen months, and he got his life turned around. It has been a miracle. He is still alive today; he probably wouldn't have been alive if he hadn't gone. It was his choice. The truth is, with anyone who does drugs or alcohol, it has to be their choice. You can't make them change. I could only say, "All of life comes to me with ease and joy and glory." Do I always believe it? Not always. But I use it because the universe hears and the universe responds.

It is our hope that you will use the tools and information in this book to generate a financial reality that is far greater than the one you presently have!

GLOSSARY

Be

In this book, we sometimes use the word be in an unconventional way, as in the question, "What generative energy, space, and consciousness can I be that would allow me to be the energy of having and accumulating money I truly be?

We use the word be here because if you can't be money, you can't have money.

Why don't we say, "the money I truly am"? Because am is an evidentiary contrivance of beingness. Am is a contrived point of view. Be refers to infinite being, where you can be all aspects of everything you could potentially be.

Clearing Statement (POD/POC)

The clearing statement we use in Access is: Right and wrong, good and bad, POD, POC, all nine, shorts, boys, and beyonds.

Right and Wrong, Good and Bad is shorthand for: What's good, perfect, and correct about this? What's wrong, mean, vicious, terrible, bad, and awful about this? What's right and wrong, good and bad? POC is the point of creation of the thoughts, feelings, and emotions immediately preceding whatever you decided. POD is the point of destruction immediately preceding whatever you decided. It's like pulling the bottom card out of a house of cards. The whole thing falls down.

All Nine stands for nine layers of crap that were taken out. You know that somewhere in those nine layers, there's got to be a pony because you couldn't put that much shit in one place without having a pony in there. It's shit that you're generating yourself, which is the bad part.

Shorts is the short version of: What's meaningful about this? What's meaningless about this? What's the punishment for this? What's the reward for this?

Boys stands for nucleated spheres. Have you ever seen one of those kids' bubble pipes? Blow here and you create a mass of bubbles? And you pop one and it fills in?

Beyonds are feelings or sensations you get that stop your heart, stop your breath, or stop your willingness to look at possibilities. It's like when your business is in the red and you get another final notice and you say argh! You weren't expecting that right now.

Sometimes, instead of saying "use the clearing statement," we just say, "POD and POC it."

Conflictual Universe
(also called a conflictual reality or a conflictual paradigm)

It's a point of view that contains conflicting elements. It's a problem. For example, were you told as a child that the love of money is the root of evil? And are you refusing to be evil? That's a conflictual universe.

Evidentiary Contrivance

It is a contrived point of view, a viewpoint you have developed. It is when you say, "This is the way money ought to be," or "This is the way things ought to work with money." You consider that you would like something to be a certain way and then you gather evidence to try and make it right. It is not looking at what is.

A Note to Readers

The information about money that is presented in this book is actually just a small taste of what Access has to offer. There is a whole universe of Access processes and classes. If there are places where you can't get things to work in your life the way you know they ought to work, you might be interested in attending an Access class or locating an Access facilitator who can work with you personally to give you greater clarity about issues you can't overcome, whether they are about money or anything else. Access processes are done with a trained facilitator and are based on the energy of you and the person you're working with.

For more information, visit: www.accessconsciousness.com

Recommended Books About Money

Money Isn't the Problem, You Are,
by Gary Douglas and Dr. Dain Heer

Prosperity Consciousness,
by Steve and Chutisa Bowman

The Penny Capitalist: How to Build a Small Fortune from Next to Nothing,
by James J. Hester

How to Get Out of Debt, Stay Out of Debt and Live Prosperously
by Jerrold Mundis

About the Authors

Gary M. Douglas

20 years ago, Gary M. Douglas started to develop Access Consciousness® with the knowing that a different way of functioning in the world must be possible. His purpose with Access is to create a world of consciousness and oneness where consciousness includes everything and judges nothing. Simple, effective, and to the point, Access is a set of tools, processes and questions that enable people to create change in any area of their life.

Born in the American Midwest and raised in San Diego, California, Mr. Douglas has always been on a spiritual path, seeking deeper answers to life's mysteries. His innate curiosity has allowed him to question what didn't seem to be working in life and to seek alternatives to the popular views and accepted wisdom of today. He has been married twice and has four children.

Today, Mr. Douglas' workshops can be found in 30 countries and is offered by over 600 facilitators worldwide. Mr. Douglas continues to travel all over the world facilitating advanced classes on subjects ranging from bodies, the Earth, animals, conscious children, possibilities, relationship, and money.

The techniques of Access Consciousness are being used worldwide to transform lives and bodies in private practices as well as in conjunction with addiction recovery, weight loss, business and money, animal health and many holistic health modalities, such as acupuncture and chiropractic care.

Mr. Douglas has written several books on the subjects of money, sex, relationship, magic and animals. In 2010, "The Place" became a Barnes and Noble best-seller.

To find out more, please visit:

www.GaryMDouglas.com
www.accesstheplace.com

Dr. Dain Heer

Dr. Dain Heer travels all over the world facilitating advanced classes on Access Consciousness.

He invites and inspires people to more consciousness from total allowance, caring, humor, and a phenomenal knowing.

Within Access, Dr. Dain Heer has developed a unique energy process for change for individuals and groups, called The Energetic Synthesis of Being. Dr. Dain Heer has a completely different approach to change. He teaches people to tap into and recognize their own abilities and knowing. The energetic transformation possible is fast --- and truly dynamic.

Dr. Heer started work as a Network Chiropractor eleven years ago in California. Having worked with bodies since he was in college, Dr. Heer came across Access Consciousness at a point in his life when he was deeply unhappy and even planning suicide. Access Consciousness changed everything. When none of the other modalities and techniques Dr. Heer had been studying were giving him lasting results or change, with Access Consciousness, his life began to expand and grow with more ease and speed than even he could have imagined possible.

Dr. Heer has written a series of books on the topics of embodiment, healing, money and relationships.

To find out more, please visit:

www.drdainheer.com
www.beingyouchangingtheworld.com

Other Books
By Gary M. Douglas & Dr. Dain Heer

The Place
By Gary M. Douglas
2010 Barnes and Noble #1 Best Selling Novel. "In this book you may find out what you have always been looking for, and how and where it may exist."

Being You, Changing the World
By Dr. Dain Heer
Have you always known that something COMPLETELY DIFFERENT is possible? What if you had a handbook for infinite possibilities and dynamic change to guide you? With tools and processes that actually worked and invited you to a completely different way of being? For you? And the world?

Divorceless Relationships
By Gary M. Douglas
A Divorceless Relationship is one where you don't have to divorce any part of you in order to be in a relationship with someone else. It is a place where everyone and everything you are in a relationship with can become greater as a result of the relationship.

Magic. You Are It. Be It.
By Gary M. Douglas & Dr. Dain Heer
Magic is about the fun of having the things you desire. The real magic is the ability to have the joy that life can be.
practice a hands-on body process that has created miraculous results all over the world!

Money Isn't The Problem, You Are
By Gary M. Douglas & Dr. Dain Heer
Offering out-of-the-box concepts with money. It's not about money. It never is. It's about what you're willing to receive.

Sex is Not a Four Letter Word but Relationship Often Times Is
By Gary M. Douglas & Dr. Dain Heer
Funny, frank and delightfully irreverent, this book offers readers an entirely fresh view of how to create great intimacy and exceptional sex.

www.accessconsciousness.com

www.isnowthetime.com

Access Workshops & Seminars

If you liked what you read in this book and are interested in attending Access seminars, workshops or classes, then for a very different point of view, read on and sample a taste of what is available. These are the core classes in Access Consciousness®

Access Bars (One day)

Facilitated by Certified Access Bars Facilitators Worldwide Bars is one of the foundational tools of Access. In this one day class, you will learn a hands-on energetic process, which you will gift and receive during the class. The Access Bars are 32 points on the head that when lightly touched clear all of the limitations you have about different areas of your life and body. These areas include money, aging, body, sexuality, joy, sadness, healing, creativity, awareness and control plus many more. What would it be like to have more freedom in all of these areas? In this one day class you will learn the basic tools of Access Consciousness® and receive and gift 2 Access Bars sessions. At worst it will feel like a great massage and at best your whole life will change!

Prerequisites: None
Access Foundation
Facilitated by Certified Access Facilitators Worldwide

Access Foundation

This two day class is about giving you the space to look at your life as a different possibility. Unlock your limitations about embodiment, finances, success, relationships, family, YOU and your capacities, and much more! Step into greater possibilities for having everything you truly desire in life as you learn tools and questions to change anything that's not working for you. You works wonders on scars and pains in the body! If you could change anything in your life, what would it be?

Prerequisites: Access Bars
Access Level 1
Facilitated by Certified Access Facilitators Worldwide

Access, Level 1

Is a two day class that shows you how to be more conscious in every area of your life and gives you practical tools that allow you to continue expanding this in your dayto-day! Create a phenomenal life filled with magic, joy and ease and clear your limitations about what is truly available for you. Discover the 5 Elements of Intimacy, create energy flows, start laughing and celebrating living and practice a hands-on body process that has created miraculous results all over the world!

Prerequisites: Access Foundation
Access Levels 2 & 3
Facilitated Exclusively by Gary M. Douglas (Founder of Access Consciousness®) and Dr. Dain Heer

Access, Levels 2 & 3

Having completed Level 1 and opened up to more awareness of you, you start to have more choice in life and become aware of what choice truly is. This four day class covers a huge range of areas including the joy of business, living life for the fun of it, no fear, courage and leadership, changing the molecular structure of things, creating your body and your sexual reality, and how to stop holding on to what you want to get rid of! Is it time to start receiving the change you've been asking for?

Prerequisites: Access Bars, Foundation and Level I

The Energetic Synthesis of Being (ESB)
Facilitated Exclusively by Dr. Dain Heer

This three day class is a unique way of working with energy, groups of people and their bodies simultaneously, created and facilitated by Dr. Dain Heer. During this class, your being, your body and the earth are invited to energetically synthesize in a way that creates a more conscious life and a more conscious planet. You begin to access and be energies you never knew were available. By being these energies, by being you, you change everything; the planet, your life and everyone you come into contact with. What else is possible then?

Prerequisites: Access Bars, Foundation and Level 1

Printed in Australia
AUOC010847280812
253681AU00001B/1/P

9 780984 783168